THE PRAYER WARRIOR

D. Tina Batten
Traci Wooden-Carlisle

THE PRAYER WARRIOR

By D. Tina Batten and Traci Wooden-Carlisle
Print ISBN 978-1-7367513-1-2

Dedication

I dedicate this book to my Lord and Saviour Jesus Christ for giving me the vision, story concept and for bringing me together with another amazing storyteller. Traci, You Rock!

Our accomplishments are HIS. To God Be The Glory!

D. Tina Batten

I dedicate this book to God, my dearest, sweetest Father, who has given me a gift that feeds my soul and blessed me with an amazing and talented friend whom He partnered me with to see His project come to fruition.

Traci Wooden Carlisle

Table of Contents

Chapter 1

For we wrestle not against flesh and blood
Ephesians 6:12

"They are not yours to keep!"

The mist settling over the earth was about five inches high. It nearly obscured the ground in front of her as far as her eyes could see. She was reminded of mud-covered battlefields with little to shield one from enemy fire.

The clouds hung low, making the whole scene look like something out of an apocalyptic dream. The fallow ground before her was vast. It was a wasteland, offering only the promise that nothing would ever grow there again. The desolation could have gone on forever, except for the demonic presence that lined itself up like a dirty barrier of windows used to dim and conceal what was on the other side.

She felt them, though. She felt each and every one of the children held in bondage on the other side of that transparent demonic force. The thought brought to mind a scripture, and she looked down at the writing on the sword in her hand. She could have spent time thinking about how odd it was that she didn't remember taking a sword with her, but there were more pressing matters, and she was happy to have the weapon to wield.

She began reading the inscribed scripture out loud, her voice ringing across the barren land slick with mud. *"For we wrestle not against flesh and blood,"*

1

As the words left her lips, they solidified in the atmosphere, charging toward their mark like a spear. They reached the barrier, causing it to shift and ripple but not tear. She kept on reading, raising her voice an octave, *"But against principalities, against powers, against the rulers of the darkness of this world, against spiritual wickedness in high places."*

She began speaking in her heavenly language, her voice ringing powerfully through the mist, dispelling the confusion.

Once again, the words appeared on the sword and as she spoke them out loud, they appeared before her in the air and raced towards their target.

She spoke each word louder and louder, giving strength to each syllable, sending it further and faster. The words went forth, each one bolder than the last, and more committed to destroying the plan of the enemy.

Her words angered the forces, and their movements became erratic. Instead of being frightened by their shift, she became emboldened and indignant, causing her voice to grow louder and more firm until she was almost shouting.

She took in a breath, preparing for her next words, then noticed she wasn't touching the ground. She was floating instead, her body not reacting to gravity. Without the ability to plant her feet, she tensed and used her diaphragm to push out the words.

As she spoke the last word, one entity broke away from the barrier, shrieking hideously and racing toward her.

"I recognize you," she said. "I call you out in the name of Jesus. The name above all names." She looked down once again at the sword in her hand and pointed it at the demon coming toward her. She began reading the new words that appeared on its blade.

"For though we walk in the flesh, we do not war after the flesh. For the weapons of our warfare are not carnal, but mighty through God to the pulling down of strongholds;"

The dark, nearly translucent being that glided towards her slowed as if it were coming up against an invisible obstacle. She grew bolder in her recitation.

"Casting down imaginations, and every high thing that exalteth itself against the knowledge of God, and bringing into captivity every thought to the obedience of Christ."

The demon came to a halt hovering over the ground twenty feet away.

"The Lord rebuke you!" she yelled, in response to its shrieks. It slowly began moving towards her. She looked down at the sword, wondering if she did something wrong. The words, *"Do not fear them, for the Lord your God is the one fighting for you"* shone brightly on the metal, almost glowing in the dim atmosphere.

His word was key in this fight. She looked up and noticed that the figure before her had stopped once again.

She looked down at the sword once again and began reading the new words that had replaced the last. *"That at the name of Jesus every knee should bow, of those in heaven, and of those on earth, and of those under the earth, and that every tongue should confess that Jesus Christ is Lord, to the glory of God the Father."*

The shrieking stopped, and she looked up in time to see the figure dissipate. It didn't blow up or make some loud sound. It quietly dissolved, pieces of it floating, then scattering in the mist. She peered beyond it at the barrier between her and the children and saw its opacity wavering.

A deep anger rose up in her, causing her to shout out, "I cast you into the dry places!" She felt, more than heard the barrier shudder, and what was left of the demonic force disappeared.

"They are not yours to keep. Release those children in Jesus name!" she cried out as she glimpsed familiar faces between the floating wall, but nothing happened. With every face that was revealed, her heart squeezed harder with pain, until she felt as if she would suffocate.

She looked down at the sword again for instruction, desperate now for the words *Name Them* were now etched upon the blade. She opened her mouth to say the first name but felt a pull near her solar plexus, as if she were being yanked backward. The scene before her became translucent, but she struggled against the pull and stepped back into place on the battlefield.

"In the name of Jesus, free Merissa Dokes," she yelled, and in a few seconds saw the child run through the barrier towards her.

In the name of Jesus, free Sebastian Spear," she called out. Another child broke away from the line and ran her way.

She called name after name, proclaiming the name of Jesus with each request. She steadied her stance and gritted her teeth against whatever was trying to pull her away from her assignment. She would resist the pull for as long as she could. She had to free those children.

She yelled out name after name until the pull disrupted her ability to use her diaphragm. Then she whispered, her hand gripping the sword tighter as she raised it as a symbol of her plight.

She spoke one last name before she was pulled from the field and launched into the darkness screaming, "the Blood of Jesus!"

***

She sat up in bed, breathing heavily, poised to yell, but the change of environment pulled the words from her mind. She gripped the sheets in her damp hands as if she were wielding a sword. She looked down expecting to see it in her hands, even as her mind began registering a different texture. Her heart beat as though she was in the middle of a sprint. She could feel that she was on the verge of running away, but didn't know if she was heading to or from something.

Her stomach was clutched tight and she felt a curl of dread wrapping around her mind. Her eyes darted back and forth in the quiet room, looking for the threat or at least the cause for her alertness. An ache took hold of her side, catching her attention. She made herself relax her abdomen and breathe deeply. She rested her head in her palms as she forced her breathing to slow. She'd been dreaming. She felt the pull on her memory, even as important details stayed just out of reach then sped further away with each second. Colors, smells and the urgency of the dream stayed, though, taunting her.

She squinted and blinked, trying to adjust her eyes to the darkness of her room. The single shaft of light coming in from a slit in the drawn curtains was no competition for the blanket of early-morning dimness surrounding her.

She breathed in deeply, hearing nothing louder than the beating of her heart for a few seconds before trying to disentangle herself from the bedclothes. She must have been extremely fitful in her sleep by the look and feel of the covers wrapped around her legs and ankles. She inspected her bare legs, half-expecting to see mud-covered armored boots on her feet and armor plating on her calves, knees and thighs. She wouldn't have been surprised to find a breastplate guarding her midsection.

She wiped at the fine sheen of sweat on her upper lip, then realized it was all over her body as well, causing her nightgown to cling to her frame. As her eyes adjusted to the dim light, she surveyed her bedding, noticing the bend and dents in her pillow, which confirmed the tight clutch she'd had upon it for quite a while.

She reached for the bottle of water she kept on her bedside table and took a swallow.

She spotted her nightcap hanging off the edge of the bed even as she reached for the crown of her head and found it bare. She tried again to remember what had caused her to struggle so much. She was able to draw essences of the dream, which caused an all-over, involuntary shiver before it escaped her mental grasp. She knew it was gone for now, but hoped throughout the day different conversations, views or feelings would trigger something. She had had such dreams many times each seemingly more intense than the last.

She sighed and drew in a deep breath, which was interrupted by the sound of her alarm clock. The sound helped to dispel the haze leftover from her dream and push her the rest of the way into reality.

She slowly shifted her body until her legs were hanging over the side of the bed. She placed both feet flat on the rug covering the floor. Then she grabbed her hair, making a quick single French braid down the middle of her head before performing her daily shoulder and neck rolls.

She turned gingerly, intentionally slowing her movements to make sure they were smooth, since her muscles were very cold and she didn't want to risk injury. Then she moved into a praying position kneeling down at her bedside.

She began her morning worship time with a fervent prayer to God, thanking Him for another day's journey. Giving thanks, praise and love for all people. Praying for the world leaders, the nation, peace, love, healing and the grace of the Lord and Savior to all mankind.

God's people were made to worship Him. They were not created to spend an eternity separated from Him in hell. She was reminded yet again that hell wasn't made for people. That statement kept ringing in her soul, so she prayed for the redemption of those still lost and hurting. She could feel their despair. It caused her to begin to utter words in her heavenly language until something broke and laughter came forth from her belly with the release of His promise.

The peace that came over her and the entire room was palpable. She wept while she praised, feeling the worship grow from the depth of her being and swell until she couldn't contain it. Even as the words left her lips, her heart lifted and the darkness around her dissipated with the passing of the first rays of light over the horizon. She lifted her slim frame from the side of the bed with an ease and quickness that belied her almost sixty years. Her movements were efficient and deliberate, giving her a sense of power and authority over her body's ability.

She changed into her daily workout clothes and got on her exercise bike as she had every other day. She glanced around her room and took in the neat and tidy space as she rode. She was proud of the place she'd carved out for herself, with God's help. The words efficacious grace came to mind and she lifted her hands in praise, shaking her head slightly, unable to voice the words echoing in her heart. There was no explaining the wealth around her. They were gifts God gave her through people He used to show her His love.

It had been a long road to this place of peace. After the loss of her child and the meltdown of her 15-year marriage which she'd prayed, cried and railed at God through, she surrendered every part of her life she hadn't already, to God.

As she inhaled the now faint scent of lavenders, she conceded that the decision to give everything to God was one of the best ones she'd ever made. She was content. Actually, more than that. She was happy and being used more than she ever thought possible. There were so many people hurting. Sometimes it was a little daunting, like this morning.

Usually her room, with the inspirational artwork that hung on the walls, as well as throughout the home, gave her the extra push she needed. The cozy and chic décor, with its warm color pallet, soothed her almost as much as God's presence did.

Only, today there was something different. It was harder to keep pace with her daily speed, and by the time she was done she had trouble catching her breath. A tiredness kept pulling at her. She ignored it and dug in deep to finish her routine, while making a quick mental note to schedule a doctor's appointment later that day for the coming week.

She continued her morning ritual. After brushing her teeth and showering, she looked at herself in the mirror, remembering to conduct self-examinations of body parts.

With one push of a button the sound from her iPod docker filled the air. She made her way down the hall to the kitchen area, and uplifting music played softly in the background while she began putting together her meals for the day.

She blended the different fruits, vegetables and powders for her healthy green breakfast smoothie. Then went about putting together her lunch, her athletic figure moving smoothly around the kitchen with an efficient grace that was lost on so many her age. She took very good care of herself, knowing that her temple was a gift from God, and unless technology made some huge leaps and bounds, it would be the only one she received. As she passed the mirror just outside of the kitchen, she took one last assessing look at her long, jet-black, wavy hair and brown skin with olive undertones. There was only a hint of crow's feet--or laugh lines, as she liked to think of them--around her eyes.

She knew many considered her an extremely attractive older woman. It was nothing new to her. She'd learned at an early age that her physical beauty could be a blessing or a curse, but coupled with the love in her heart and the wisdom in her soul, it was an easy way to gain someone's attention simply to offer a warm smile of greeting, or break the ice in situations where she was prompted to deliver a word.

She grabbed all of the personal items she needed for the day as she walked to the front door. As she passed the numerous framed diplomas and certifications of achievement hanging on the wall, all displaying the name Beatrice Isadora Vacherchesse, she could imagine her mother and father looking down upon her proudly.

Spying some dust on top of one of the frames, she ran her finger along it for a few inches and came away with an embarrassing amount of dirt. She winced, wondering if her parents caught that as well.

She told herself that she would give the area a good cleaning when she got home. As she entered her foyer, she picked her keys up from a small table that held a pair of gold dipped baby booties with the name Victoria etched along the front of the plaque attached to the tiny shoes. As she did every day, she ran her fingers lovingly along the tongues and toes of the shoes before she walked through the door, shutting it behind her.

She paused to do a mental scan of everything she carried: her green shake in a to-go container; her purse, which hung off of one shoulder; her car and door keys, which she held in her hand; and her briefcase, which hung off the other shoulder. Feeling confident that she had everything, she crossed the distance from her door to her vehicle, but as she slipped the key in the door lock, she noticed the smudge of dirt left over from her finger. She looked up sheepishly, "Sorry, Mama." Then giggled as she slid inside and pressed the button to lock the doors of her sedan.

As she pulled out of her driveway, Ms. V. considered how blessed she was to have a home that was both her shelter and sanctuary. Her heart longed to go back, but she had a feeling today was going to be full of new experiences and she could expect the unexpected.

Choose ye, this day... she said under her breath, proclaiming the victory of the day as hers right before she put her car in drive.

Chapter 2

Suffer little children to come unto me, and forbid them not: for of such is the kingdom of God.
Matthew 19:14

"If only these walls could talk"

As Ms. V. drove up to the block-wide building, she considered how quickly she'd made it to work. She must have had a great deal on her mind to arrive without noticing the normal stop and go of traffic that usually accompanied her to work each day.

She pulled into the employee parking lot beside the two-story structure that housed the main part of the Center of Hope Christian Academy (COHCA). One other small building sat on each side of the main building. One housed the wood, photo, and auto shops, and the other housed the gymnasium, which was used for basketball, volleyball, and tennis. The field used for baseball and soccer was behind the main building, which made securing the student parking lot and building easier. The main building held an auditorium, classrooms, the teacher's lounge, the administrative offices, a small infirmary and Ms. V's counseling office.

The school was filled with a wide variety of students from every background and economic status. As Ms. V. walked through the hallway to the administrative office, she was greeted by many teens. The "Hey Ms. V.", "What's up Ms. V." and "Good morning," brought a smile to her face.

She smiled back at a few of the students, greeting them with a "Blessings be upon you." To one student in particular, she said, "Looking forward to seeing you later today."

"Okay Ms. V, I won't be late for my appointment."

It touched her heart to have so many students greet her. Her response, "Blessings be upon you," readily upon her lips, was her way of giving them acknowledgment of the spiritual favor they possessed as children of the Most High God.

Ms. V. walked into the administrative office and greeted everyone with her cheery demeanor, which was uplifting to most of the occupants. Well, pretty much all except one.

"It's way too early for all that noise," mumbled Myra, the receptionist.

She cut her eyes at Ms. V., with the constant sour expression that had etched lines around her mouth, making her look older than she actually was.

Ms. V. chose to ignore the woman's less-than-welcoming remark. She'd been at the school long enough to hear the different stories about Myra and her past.

From what she had heard, the young woman seemed to go through one disappointing relationship after the other. Myra, however, also seemed to foster an anger and bitterness that she used to shield herself from the emotional attachments even as she sought them. It was ironic, really, that while working at a Christian Academy Myra wouldn't take advantage of the opportunity her work environment afforded her. She could be healed if she could trust in God enough to open the fortress she'd built around her heart, and let the bridge down over the moat she used to discourage any inadvertent trespassers.

Meanwhile, Ms. V. would continue to speak words of kindness, hoping one day Myra would be able to feel the love behind her words and receive the gift she offered freely. Ms. V. smiled to herself, thankful for the gift of discernment that allowed her to see through some of the expressions of hurt and pain people used as defense mechanisms. Life was so much more pleasant when you didn't feel the need to take certain things personally.

"What are you so happy about?" Myra said, snapping Ms. V, out of her thoughts. She heard the underlying envy in the woman's voice and considered how to answer her question without sounding like she was bragging as she checked her box for messages. She didn't have to think too long.

"Wish my world was like yours," Myra continued, mostly under her breath, but still just loud enough for Ms. V. to hear. "I don't know what there is to be so happy about."

Ms. V. hesitated only a second before responding, "There's always something to be happy about. The Lord woke you up this morning. You still have breath in your body. As long as those two things keep happening, you have the chance to choose to be happy, to choose to be thankful for all the things you have been blessed with."

Myra winced as if the words affected her physically, "I'm just not into all of that spiritual stuff right now."

Remember her training to not only be slow to speak, but to value the power in words, Ms. V. hesitated, calling back words that may have harmed rather than helped. She always tried to listen twice before speaking. First to the person and second to the Holy Spirit. Myra was so focused on her pain and anger that any talk about happiness she could be missing would only hurt her. "I'm am going to continue to pray for you, Myra."

Myra shrugged her shoulders looking up at Ms. V. with anger in her eyes, "Can't stop you."

Ms. V. mimicked the young woman's movements. "No. You can't."

"Do what you need to do," Myra said before returning her attention to the paperwork on her desk.

Before leaving the administrative office, Ms. V. called over her shoulder a sincere, "Blessings be upon you."

Myra waved her hand and rolled her eyes before reaching for the office phone that started to ring. She then turned her high back, black leather office chair around to politely answer the phone.

As she walked from the office Ms. V. could hear the change in Myra's voice as she spoke a greeting into the receiver. "Good morning, Center of Hope Christian Academy, how may I help you sir or madam?"

As she closed the door behind her and made her way to her office, Ms. V. prayed that the Lord would soften Myra's hardened heart. She was resolved herself to keep her word. She would continue to pray for Myra. The woman was worth more than the anger and bitterness she surrounded herself with.

She proceeded to walk down the hallway towards her office when she felt a pull on her spirit, causing her to gaze around her with more purpose.

Arriving at her office door after greeting a few more students along the way, Ms. V.'s heartbeat picked up as she spied one particular student in the crowd moving down the hall in her direction. The urgency from the early morning dream gripped her as she watched the child get closer.

"Hi Ms. V."

"Sebastian," she said, feeling a sense of déjà vu. "How are you doing? Did you have a good weekend?"

The boy shrugged unconvincingly. "Okay."

"We can talk about it today." She responded.

"I'm scheduled for today?" He asked frowning slightly, then smiling sheepishly. If she wasn't mistaken, he looked as though he was relieved at the idea.

"Yes, you are." She leaned slightly against the wall next to her door as the feeling of déjà vu moved through her.

"I will see you after fifth period," she said, continuing to watch his expressions closely, looking for something…she wasn't sure of what, but it hovered on the edge of her conscious thought.

"Good," he replied after a couple of seconds. His features cleared, dispelling the hold on her senses.

He continued down the hall and she watched him until he was swallowed up by the crowd.

Ms. V. turned back to her door and reached for the lock. She glanced down, noticing the piece of leather peeking out from her shirt sleeve. She didn't remember putting her old I.D. bracelet on that morning. She studied its leather form and ran her fingers across the almost-smooth etched letters as she had so many times since her parents had given it to her on her sixteenth birthday. The bracelet didn't go with her outfit, so she thought she had left it in her jewelry box.

"Mmm"

The more she puzzled over it, the heavier her shoulders seemed to get, planting her to the spot. She felt arrested and as though she were suspended between two worlds.

"Are you alright?"

The voice drew her back to the present, and she looked up to find Mr. Sanderson watching her with a quizzical expression.

"Good morning, Mr. Sanderson." Ms. V pulled at her sleeve self-consciously.

"Are you alright?" he repeated.

"Um," She looked down at the key in her hand, then back up at the Center of Hope's head science teacher. "Yes, I am. Just felt a little winded for a moment there. I'm good now. How are you on this fine morning?"

Mr. Sanderson looked a little surprised by her question, but answered all the same. "I'm good. Thank you."

She nodded. "Wonderful. Blessings be upon you, Mr. Sanderson."

"And you, Ms. V." He replied and slowly stepped away.

She didn't hesitate before unlocking her door. The click seemed to come from far away, and she placed her hand on the door jamb to steady herself. Her senses went on alert, but not with a fight or flight impulse. She felt as though she'd been given a jolt of electricity. Every one of her senses were operating at two hundred percent. Her sense of smell was heightened, and she caught a whiff of the cleanser the janitor used on the grout between the tiles and baseboards. Her arms tingled beneath her jacket, making her feel as though she were wearing little more than a T-shirt in the drafty hall. Her hearing picked up sounds not normally associated with a school hall full of children, and she squeezed her eyes shut against the sudden glare coming through the window at the end of the corridor. The overload made her feel lightheaded for a couple of seconds, then everything righted itself and she was back in front of her door with one hand on the jamb and the other on the knob.

Why am I standing in the doorway as if frozen in time?

She turned the knob and pushed the door open. She took a few steps inside the office and her strides faltered. Her heart hammered in her chest as it absorbed the remnants of eight years of emotional counseling that continued to flood the hallways of the Academy. How much the world had changed.

She moved forward even more cautiously, but when she didn't experience another episode, she went about getting her room ready for the day's counseling sessions.

Ms. V. moved to the window behind her desk. The sound her wedged shoes made on the tile had an odd echo in the furniture-laden room. She opened the blinds and closed her eyes as the rays of the sun warmed her face, reminding her of the warmth and peace she normally felt when she walked in her office. She'd spent a great deal of her time in this room, and had some things upgraded to suit the needs of those who came in for counseling.

After the first few months she knew the stark white walls weren't going to work. They were too sterile, and made the office look like every other classroom. She'd asked the principal if she could add a few luxuries to allow people to relax. She was told that there was no budget for upgrades, but if she followed the code, she could have the wall color changed and the floor upgraded if she paid for it.

Most people might have become disgruntled and discouraged, but Ms. V. felt just the opposite. She had been given permission to soften the environment and she did exactly that.

The walls were now a cross between off-white and the lightest shade of blue the naked eye could detect. She'd always felt as though blue was a soothing color, but it would have stood out too much in its undiluted form. She wasn't there to make waves, but to help heal the student body and staff.

A sturdy cotton runner in earth tones, accented with splashes of light blue, ran the distance between the door and the two rather comfortable brown pleather chairs in front of her desk. The runner kept the dirt from foot traffic to a minimum and served as a welcome mat at the door, reminding people they had just entered a comforting and safe environment. It had been a recommendation from maintenance when she'd had the room upgraded with the beige and cream tile, and she was happy she followed their advice. It was worth the extra work it took to roll up the rug and carry it to the laundromat once every semester.

This office had been a great deal of her world for the past eight years. She looked around the room, proud of the display of accomplishments on the walls. Accomplishments -of so many students and faculty she had counseled over the years.

"If only these walls could talk" she whispered while scanning some of the shelves with figurines and knickknacks gifted to her over the years. "The stories they could tell." she murmured as she ran her fingers lovingly over a red apple made of glass. She kept her office much the same way as she kept her home; every item was back in its rightful place by the end of each day.

She walked around the room, taking in the curio cabinet in the corner under the window, the maple shelving unit against the far wall, and the oversized plush chair and small glass table in the corner opposite to her desk. She used it as a quiet corner. There were small mementos along the surfaces given to her from students, past and present showing their appreciation for her words of honest wisdom and pure encouragement and positivity, and how she helped them from a moment of crisis to clarity. They were each symbols of gratitude for the love she had shown them over the years; the many talks with no judgment, just pure love.

Many times, she would encourage people to make themselves comfortable. To some, it meant taking off their jackets and scarves, to others it meant taking off their shoes.

She noticed the sound of slow rhythmic beeping and looked around for the cause, but just as quickly as it came, there was nothing but silence. It struck a chord in her, reminding her of what she'd overlooked.

She'd been so preoccupied by everything she'd dreamed that morning, and maybe imagined when she first placed her key in the lock, that she'd forgone her daily ritual of praying over everything seen and unseen in her office.

She closed her eyes and took a deep breath as she focused on His presence. She ran her hands lovingly across the backs of the pleather chairs facing her desk as she prayed God's love and peace would saturate them. She remembered sitting in both of the chairs in the store for several minutes, praying before deciding to purchase them.

She prayed over the knick-knacks on her desk that seemed to draw most people to touch. She prayed over the books on the shelves that more nervous or antsy children would scan or touch while they were trying to think of what to say. She prayed over the plants she sprayed with water every other day that were placed around the room. She even prayed over her computer, but that was more for her benefit than for the piece of antiquated equipment.

She needed to get her day started, but before she had a chance to warm her seat, there was a knock at her door.

Chapter 3

Let your manner of living be without covetousness, and be content with such things as ye have. For He hath said, "I will never leave thee, nor forsake thee"
Hebrews 13:5

"The world has it twisted."

The knocking stopped for a moment and was replaced with the sound of a louder-than-usual conversation going on outside of her door. She checked the clock. Classes wouldn't start for another fifteen minutes. As the conversation grew louder the grief in the young lady's voice reached out to Ms. V. She had just placed her hands on the armchair to lift herself up when the knocking continued then stopped for a couple of seconds. She was about to call out when it came again, almost incessantly. The doorknob turned, and she wondered if the person on the other side heard the permission she was trying to give. A young lady with a tear-streaked face peeked around the door. Ms. V. gestured for her to come in.

Porcha stood by the door she'd just shut, shifting from one foot to the other.

"I have excellent hearing, but don't you think it would be easier to talk if you came closer?" Ms. V. punctuated her invitation by pushing the tissue box on her desk closer to one of the chairs directly in front of it. The young lady made her way to the seat in front of the tissue box and sat down.

She waited patiently as the girl blew her nose and wiped her eyes.

"Ms. V. I need to talk," Porcha said after gaining some composure.

Ms. V. merely nodded. "Before we begin. Let's pray. Dear Lord, thank you for being with us always. Thank you for being ever mindful of us and holding our every concern in your hands. I ask that you comfort your daughter Porcha. Pour out your peace upon her and give her clarity. Keep your hedge of protection around her and her family. Give me the words you wish her to hear and seal our conversation with your Holy Spirit." She silently thanked God for drawing young people to her, and she was honored.

She could hear Porcha's agreement as the young lady echoed her words of thanks.

Ms. V. watched patiently as Porcha sat rolling the tissue around her forefinger. Tears still rolled down her cheeks, but she seemed too preoccupied with her thoughts to realize. Ms. V. saw Porcha's deep inhale get interrupted by a hiccup and knew the emotional turmoil that brought the water works to the surface was deep.

"I, uh, I have a problem."

Ms. V. continue to keep an open expression on her face.

"I thought my boyfriend Kevin and I had an understanding." Porcha dabbed at her eyes, sending a stab of pain through Ms. V.'s heart when she looked up with heartbreak clearly written on her face.

"We were going to wait until marriage for sex, but lately he's been hinting at more. Well, more than hinting actually. More like groping." She said the last more to herself than Ms. V., returning her eyes to the tissue.

Ms. V. silently continued to pray for the young girl and for what to say to her that would bring comfort and remind her of the vow she'd taken.

The Center of Hope Academy held a Fathers & Daughters Purity Dance. It was a celebration of the relationship between fathers and daughters, as well as their shared endeavor to encourage communication and reinforce the vow the daughters made to abstain from sex. Porcha and her father had attended counseling sessions before, as well as the dance, where he presented her with a ring to symbolize her vow to remain celibate.

No one believed it would be easy, but the school tried to give both father and daughter as many weapons as possible to help assist her with peer pressure.

"I just feel like he's wearing me down. It's so much easier to remember the scriptures and hear God's voice when I'm away from the temptation of him."

Ms. V. hadn't said a word, but this young lady was working through her crisis smoothly. Sometimes it just took an open and objective ear.

"But shouldn't I be able to be stronger with him? Shouldn't I be able to trust him not to tempt me, let alone pressure me? I mean, he was there at the dance. He knows my vows." She threw up her hands in exasperation. "He went through the Men of Valor ceremony. He gave vows of his own, but still... Still." Ms. V. saw her swallow the rest of the words. "I love him," Porcha said through a fresh set of tears. "I don't want to lose him, but I don't know what will happen if we stay together."

Ms. V. waited for a few deep breaths before speaking, in case Porcha had more to say.

"You've been talking about your relationship with Kevin, and I understand your struggle, but what have you been talking to Jesus about lately?"

Porcha bit her lower lip for a moment, a sign Ms. V. had come to understand as Porcha's way of considering whether or not to exaggerate the truth.

"I can't help you if you don't tell me the truth." Ms. V. reminded her softly.

Porcha let out a deep breath.

"I haven't really been talking to Jesus. I mean. I say my prayers in the morning and before I go to sleep, but He's gone quiet. I don't hear Him like I used to." Porcha's sniffles turned back into sobs.

"Sshh, honey calm down. Why does this make you cry so hard?"

"I think He's left me. It used to be so easy to talk to Him."

"Ahh. No. God has promised never to leave us nor forsake us, and He has yet to break any of His promises. I am absolutely sure He wouldn't begin with you, especially if you've been wanting to talk to Him."

"Then why can't I hear Him?" Porcha asked in a near whine.

"Let's see. How much time do you spend in devotion and quiet meditation?"

Porcha began to look sheepish. "Well, since I've started driving I've had to take my little brother to school and soccer practice so I have to leave the house a half hour earlier, but I want to give more time at night and I try to wait to hear Him before I fall asleep."

"Wait for Him?" Ms. V. asked as she tried to keep up with Porcha's conversation.

"Yes. Wait for Jesus to talk to me like He used to when I first got saved. He was always right there waiting." Porcha's words were almost adamant.

Ms. V. was impressed by the teen's diligence towards keeping the lines of communication open between herself and God. She wanted to give the young lady both encouragement and instruction on how to focus on God's voice despite all of the distractions.

"He's still there, but there are times when He will purposefully get quieter so that He can get your undivided attention," Ms. V. replied.

"Why?" Porcha asked without hesitation.

"To draw you closer, and to help you weed out all of the insignificant noises so you can concentrate on Him," Ms. V. said matter-of-factly.

Porcha looked as though she were contemplating Ms. V.'s words, so she decided to make it more personal.

"Say you had something to say to your boyfriend. Kevin, right?"

"Right."

Ms. V. had Porcha's undivided attention now.

"Let's say he was watching a game on television." Ms. V. said.

"Like baseball?" Porcha said wrinkling her nose as she made the suggestion.

"Sure," Ms. V. said, working her mouth a moment to keep from laughing. "He's watching the game and you want to talk. You call his name, his body shifts towards you and he responds verbally, but his eyes are still on the game. He's giving you some attention but not his undivided attention."

Porcha's eyes lit up. "He's done that."

Oh, dear child. That is nothing to be excited about. "You may start talking to him but, how much of your conversation do you think he will remember?" Ms. V. asked

"Not much at all," Porcha said glumly.

"You may keep calling his name to let him know that you would like his undivided attention, but what if he doesn't give it to you?"

Porcha shrugged. "I would just get up and leave." Her mouth opened and closed, then opened again before she spoke again. "Do you think Jesus left because I wouldn't give Him my undivided attention?"

"No. I say again, He will never leave you nor forsake you, but at the same time, He won't be pushed idly aside. He will do things to get your attention. Sometimes His voice will get softer because what He has to tell you is important and He needs your undivided attention. What I'm saying is, I believe Jesus is trying to get your attention. If your mind is full of what's going on in school, at home and with Kevin, it's a wonder He can get a word in. Try clearing your mind of everything but Him and don't give Him a deadline for when you need Him to talk to you. Patiently wait for Him. He has been patiently waiting for you."

Porcha began nodding in agreement.

"Okay. Do you want to talk about Kevin now?" Ms. V. asked.

Porcha's eyes were bright and clear. "I'm not sure what to do."

"What do you want, Porcha?" Ms. V. asked directly.

Porcha thought over the question for few moments. "I want us to talk and be like we were when we first started going out. We have a lot in common, but the subject has been turning more and more towards sex."

"What do you do when that happens?" Ms. V. asked.

Porcha hugged herself. "Sometimes I change the subject and sometimes not."

"I'm going to tell you something that you will be able to take with you for the rest of your life," Ms. V. said, leaning forward conspiratorially. Porcha leaned in closer as well. "You need to train people how to treat you."

"Wait, what?" Porcha asked almost as quickly.

"If you give in to people even when you don't want to, you are telling them that they can convince you to do things you don't want to do. If you say 'no' and they keep pushing, then they aren't looking out for you and your best interest. A person who loves you won't contradict their words with their actions. Their first concern will be your well-being and happiness. If not..." She let the sentence fade so Porcha could think on her answer.

Porcha looked slightly crestfallen but gave Ms. V. a small smile. "So, you're saying since he keeps pressuring me, he doesn't care for me?"

"No. I'm sure he cares for you, but what he wants may not be what's best for you."

Porcha nodded. "I thought so, but I was hoping I was wrong."

"There is no in-between in life. Things are either right or wrong—black or white—and the gray area is a place of compromise." Ms. V.'s voice was firm, yet quiet. "The world has twisted it. It has tried to convince us that right is wrong and vice versa."

Porcha heaved a sigh but it seemed the waterworks were gone.

"Okay, thank you, Ms. V.," Porcha said, and began to gather her things.

"Is that it?" Ms. V. asked, a little confused about Porcha's seemingly easy acceptance of her advice.

Porcha gave her a slightly watery smile. "Yeah, um, yes."

Ms. V. took in Porcha's countenance and recognized that the hopeless was gone from her essence. Realization came over her like a wave. It wasn't Kevin the teen was heartsick over. It was her belief that the Lord had stopped speaking to her; that He had left her.

She smiled gently at the young lady whose precious heart beat for God.

"The second thing you need to take with you today is the scripture Hebrews 13:5," said Ms. V. *"Let your manner of living be without covetousness, and be content with such things as ye have. For He hath said, "I will never leave thee, nor forsake thee.* "God will never leave you nor forsake you. It is a promise He will never break. If you can't hear Him, then draw closer to Him by praying, reading His word, thinking on what He's done for you and what you love about Him."

Porcha juggled her belongings slightly and smiled again. "Thank you, Ms. V."

"My pleasure, Porcha." Ms. V. responded sincerely. She felt comfortable in the thought that Porcha had not only heard her, but would use some of the tools she'd given her during their session.

She watched the young lady turn and walk out of her office and took a deep breath, expelling some of the intensity in the room. Then she breathed in the sweet presence of God, basking in the feeling of accomplishment that came from hearing the Holy Spirit whisper His approval.

She smiled to herself and leaned back in her chair for a heartbeat. She thought it odd when she heard the next two heartbeats rather than feeling them when she placed her hand on her chest. Almost as soon as she heard the sound clearly, it was gone.

She looked around the room, feeling as though she wasn't alone, and reached out with all of her senses, but the sound of the opening school bell distracted her. When the room was quiet again the feeling was gone, and everything was back to normal.

The knock at her door moments later made her feel slightly uneasy, but she answered. "Please come in."

A man stepped in holding a beautiful bouquet of flowers in one hand and a clipboard in the other. "Are you Ms. Ver, Verache…se." He looked up from the clipboard, his face going red with embarrassment.

"Ms. V. is fine. My name can be a mouthful."

He walked to her with a grateful smile. "Well, then these must be for you." He placed the vase of colorful flowers on her desk and handed her his clipboard to sign. She smiled at him, signed it, and handed it back.

"Blessings be upon you," she said, when he turned to go. He stopped to turn back to her giving her a startled glance that morphed into a smile that warmed his eyes.

"Thank you," he said, before turning back around and walking out of the door.

She looked back down at the bouquet, studying the colors and taking in the fragrance. She reached for and grasped the note, feeling slightly disconnected from the digits holding the card.

It read, *Thank you for all of your help. Ms. V. You're the Greatest! Love Shelly.*

Ms. V. smiled and felt her heart swell then clench. It did her proud to know that some of her students were still thinking about her even after they'd left the Academy.

She blinked a few times to get her bearings, and reached for the phone on her desk. It was time to make that call to her doctor.

She placed her hand on the receiver just as the phone rang. She picked it up and was surprised to hear Myra's voice. "Ms. V. There is a delivery man coming to bring you flowers."

"Thank you, Myra, he just left."

"Mmmm. More flowers, huh. Your students must really love you."

"Yes. Kindness towards people goes a long way." Ms. V. responded. Blessing be upon you," she said before hanging up.

Chapter 4

But the fruit of the Spirit is   love,   joy,   peace,   longsuffering,
gentleness, goodness, faith, meekness, temperance: against such there is
no law.
Galatians 5:22-23

"It's none of our business."

The morning continued in a blur of paperwork, meetings and sessions with students. No day was typical, because her line of work was full of unique experiences with unique personalities. But that day felt oddly familiar. She chalked it up to a continuation of her reaction to the room earlier that morning and her slightly-off biorhythm.

The bell rang, dismissing everyone for lunch just as Ms. V. finished feeding her fish. Ms. V. placed her book of daily devotionals she'd left out in her desk drawer and put her sweater on over her blouse. The teacher's lounge was always a little drafty.

There was a quick knock on her door, and in walked her good friend Madison, holding a plant with a bright yellow bow.

"Hi there, beautiful woman of God," Madison said, and Ms. V. took in the younger woman's overall appearance.

Though there seemed to be something she was trying to hide in the depth of her dark brown eyes, Madison smiled at her brightly.   Ms. V. always admired her friend's smooth dark caramel-colored skin. Not only did it make her friend look younger than her fifty-two years, but it also reminded her of an expensive face cream ad for women. She'd seen airbrushed pictures of young women's faces that didn't look as smooth. Madison's African-American and Latin heritage showed up equally in her face and body. Her wavy hair, full lips and the straight and narrow bridge of her nose over slightly flared nostrils made it hard to tell at first glance which nationality she favored, but the temper that sometimes matched the heat in her dark, doe-like eyes tipped the scale towards her Latin ancestry. Though Ms. V. was a couple of inches taller than Madison, her friend's choice of clothing often turned her more rounded figure into a svelte physique that understated her curves. Maddison was warm, generous and fiercely protective of those who couldn't fend for themselves. Her passionate nature tended to get the best of her, but her heart was in the right place. Ms. V. had prayed often that her friend's overprotective instincts would be tempered by her love for God and her desire to obey Him by seeking the Holy Spirit before she reacted. She was still praying.

"Blessings be upon you, my friend. What's that for?" Ms. V. glanced at the plant Madison placed on the coffee table in the lounge area as she retrieved her purse from her drawer. She pulled the purse strap on her shoulder and walked towards one of her best friends in the world.

"It's just a little something I thought would brighten up your room, but I can see I'm not the first person to bring you something colorful today." Madison gestured to the bouquet of flowers sitting on Ms. V's desk.

"What can I say? I'm loved. How are you doing today?"

"I'm good," Madison said, as they exchanged hugs.

Ms. V. leaned back but didn't fully let go of her friend. Instead she scrutinized her face, which was slightly puffy.

"I'm blessed," Madison said. It was as if she were trying to convince both of them of her wellbeing, but her forced smile said something different. "I'm healthy and I serve a faithful God." Her voice wavered and her eyes watered.

"Yes, we do," Ms. V. said, placing a hand on her friend's shoulder. "Would you like to talk about it?" Ms. V., halted her friend's movements as she turned to exit the room.

"It's just…" Madison looked as though she was having trouble keeping her composure, but she took a deep breath, seeming to force back the tears. I just need you to pray in agreement with me, Beatrice, for a good friend of mine." Madison sniffed.

"Sure. What am I praying in agreement for?" Ms. V. gestured for her friend to sit in the oversized chair catty-corner to the couch that in front of the coffee table.

"I have a friend who has been undergoing a great deal of medical challenges lately. She's in a place where she can't pray for herself, which is a shame since she is one of the most powerful prayer warriors I know." Madison looked up at Ms. V. "You two would have the demonic world scrambling for cover." She smiled a little. "Right now, she is fighting for her life and I can't do anything but pray, so I need your help. I don't doubt that my prayers are reaching God's ears, but He seems to have a special affinity for you." Madison smiling fondly at her.

"I will definitely pray for the healing of your friend. Is there anything else your friend needs? Is there something that needs resolving spiritually as well?"

"You know. I'm not sure. She's always been a proverbial powerhouse when it comes to praying for people's healing, salvation, and spiritual warfare. It's like she is one of the greatest soldiers in the world, but she needs rescuing." Distress was evident in Madison's features.

"Alright then. Let us go to the Lord in prayer." Ms. V. took Madison's hand and bowed her head.

"Dear Lord. We come before your throne of grace and mercy with boldness, humbly requesting help for your daughter in Zion. We praise you and magnify your name, Oh Lord. We thank you for giving us the desire to acknowledge You in all things because in You is life and love and everything good. We thank you for who you are in our lives and that we can partake in the blessings of you." She squeezed Madison's hand again.

"Your word says, where two or three are gathered together in your name, you are in the midst of them. Heavenly Father, we ask that you touch and heal our sister in Christ. She is a great warrior of yours and is a great benefit to the advancement of the kingdom of heaven. I pray in agreement with my sister, Madison. Please pour out your spirit of peace upon her. Comfort her and give her the strength needed to continue to intercede for her friend and give me the strength to do the same. In Jesus' name we pray. Amen."

Ms. V. opened her eyes to see tears rolling down her friend's cheeks. Her heart kicked up and she involuntarily squeezed Madison's hand again. Her friend's smile was tremulous but hopeful all the same. Ms. V. sighed in relief.

Madison stood up and pulled on her hand. "Thank you so much. Come on. Let's go to lunch while there still might be a seat in the teacher's lounge."

Ms. V. got up slowly and followed her friend out of the door.

They made a side trip to the women's restroom so Madison could wash her face and reapply her makeup. Then they walked down the mostly-empty hall to the teacher's lounge.

After retrieving their lunch bags from the refrigerator, Ms. V. and Madison settled at a table near the center of the room.

As she had done many times before, Myra came into the room on her phone, rushing around and weaving her way between chairs and tables with a frantic energy that set Ms. V's teeth on edge. She closed her eyes and sought the peace that would allow her to pray over her meal and then ignore the woman's agitated state.

"Again. I ask at what point in our relationship did you start to indulge in this idea?" Myra asked, her voice growing angry. There was a pause as she listened to the person's response on the other line.

"Really?" She paused again. "So, you thought I would be okay with you investing some of the money I've been saving for our wedding in what sounds to me like a development scheme?" She paused again, and if she had any presence of mind, she would have noticed that her pause left the entire lunchroom silent.

Myra began talking again, her voice growing louder and louder until there was no room for any other conversation in the lounge.

"You are amazing. Scratch that. You are ridiculous, but your ignorance is amazing." Myra finished at a near growl. She paced back and forth, obstructing the path to the counter that housed the coffee machine, plasticware and microwave.

Mr. McNeely watched Myra with an intensity that rivaled the concentration she'd seen on children's faces when playing video games.

He waited until Myra reached one end of the counter, then he hopped up and dashed towards the plasticware to swipe a spoon from the organizer, just narrowly escaping before Myra walked back. It reminded Ms. V. of a game of double Dutch, where a person had to wait for the rope to reach the perfect position before they could jump in. Mr. McNeely was that person.

Ms. V. shook her head at the absurdity of the moment. This woman was holding people hostage with her phone call and selfishness.

Myra stopped mid-stride. She bent over, with one hand on her hip and the other holding the phone in front of her face. She spoke into the phone as if she were staring down at the person on the other end.

"I want you to replace every penny you took from my account by the end of today, or you can take every scrap of clothing and personal item you own out of my apartment." Her voice deepened to just above a growl. The next words were precisely measured, with an over-pronunciation of vowels and consonants. "Hear what I say. When I get home, your presence or complete absence will be my answer to whether or not I sue your..." Ms. V. closed her ears to the word she heard coming.

The gasps in the room were the only noises anyone had made during Myra's conversation.

Madison glanced at Ms. V. from across the table with a disgusted expression, making it clear what she thought of Myra's performance.

Ms. V. felt for Myra. Her eyes went back to the woman as Myra glanced around the room, realization dawning that everyone had heard her side of the conversation. She seemed to draw in on herself.

Ms. V. could tell that everyone's eyes were following Myra as she walked back down to the other side of the counter to the microwave, wondering if there would be an encore to go with their salads, sandwiches and soups. Myra took her lunch out of the microwave, picked up her bottle of water, and made a move to exit the teacher's lounge. She jostled Ms. V.'s chair as she walked by and Ms. V. resisted the urge to say anything. Instead, she looked down at the lunch she'd laid out on the table, considering it with a little confusion. There was chicken noodle soup, graham crackers, applesauce and - she picked up the container- what looked to be strawberry Jell-O.

Had she picked up someone else's lunch bag? She looked closer at the canvas, thermal pouch. She didn't remember adding these items to her lunch that morning. With one more glance at the items, she shrugged and dug in. She was used to seeing a little more green in her meal, but they were all good choices. She wanted to pat herself on the back for her treat to herself.

"What would it cost you to be nice?"

The tone in Madison's voice startled Ms. V. more than the words themselves, though they were odd. She looked up to find Madison staring in Myra's direction. She turned toward Myra in time to see her stop and pivot in the middle of the lounge.

Oh no.

"Are you speaking to me?" Myra asked.

"Yes," Madison said, not backing down.

Myra's mouth shut.

Ms. V. could foresee this getting out of hand very quickly. She tried to raise herself from the chair, but her legs wouldn't work. Madison's legs had no such problem—she stood up and looked in Myra's direction.

"You walk in here on your phone, weaving between chairs and seats, knocking into people without giving a care or a courteous word for the disruption you're causing. Would it really cost you so much to be nice?" Madison's voice was passionate and filled with a hurt that had nothing to do with Myra's recent misjudgment.

Ms. V. could feel the tension in the room grow.

"What do you think you would lose by being courteous?" she continued. "How hard would it be to see outside of yourself and around your pain? How hard would it be to consider that someone else might be having a bad day and are seeking the relative quietness and peace of this lounge to regroup before going back in and amongst those children? Those children who need a teacher who is attentive, clear of mind and ready to guide and pray for them at a moment's notice. They don't need teachers filled with tension and restlessness because they had to sit in the lounge during their lunch hour listening to you go off on your partner. It's none of our business, but you continue to make it our business with your loud conversation. This is a public place. Nobody wants to hear what should be a private discussion."

Ms. V.'s. heart dropped to her stomach. If she had been able to get Madison's attention, she would have stopped her friend's tirade.

She watched as Myra looked around the room, her bottom lip trembling. Then she pressed her lips together and raised her chin before stomping out of the teacher's lounge, reminding Ms. V. of a defiant child.

The quietness of the room was almost claustrophobic, and Ms. V. blew out a breath to try to release some of the tension that had been growing inside her. Everyone was looking around at one another, but no one wanted to be the first to say anything about the confrontation they'd just witnessed.

Ms. V. took a sip of her soup as she considered the words she was about to speak. Madison was her best friend, and for good reason. The woman was bold, but usually kind, and always willing to take constructive criticism. Mrs. V. knew the emotional turmoil her friend was going through, especially after her request for prayer, but a hurting Madison was more inclined to listen to God's voice than a hurting Myra. As if Madison heard her thoughts, her friend turned to her.

"Am I right? No one wanted to hear her conversation or her language." Madison looked at her plaintively, obviously expecting Ms. V. to agree. When Ms. V.'s response was slow to come, Madison frowned.

Ms. V. raised her hand when her friend opened her mouth.

"I'm not saying that what you said was wrong. I just think your words could have been said in a more loving or kind manner." Ms. V. moved her chair close to Madison's and placed her hand on her friend's hand in request for her full attention when she saw that Madison really wanted to respond. She spoke as low as she could, with the assurance that her friend could hear her.

"No one would argue that Myra was in the wrong. She was basically holding the teachers in this lounge hostage. I thought poor Mr. McNeely was going to start bobbing back and forth while he waited for enough space to get his spoon from the organizer." Ms. V. was glad to see Madison's brief smile since she'd brought up her fellow colleague's predicament simply for that reason.

"Usually you are the last one to call someone out in the middle of a crowd," Ms. V. said, approaching the initial conversation again. "I know you know better than most how volatile a situation can get when a person feels cornered, no matter how wrong they know they are." Ms. V. paused as she watched for her friend's reaction. "Myra's moves, conversations and reactions are motivated by her emotions. It's obvious she is having a hard time right now, which gives us an opening to show her God's compassion, tenderness and kindness." Ms. V. hoped her friend could see her concern.

Ms. V. removed her hand but kept her friend's gaze. "I know your concern for your friend has you on edge and in pain as well, but if we can't rise above our pain and place our trust in God so we may help those who don't know who to go to for help, we are no better." Ms. V. saw the storm in Madison's eyes just before they began to water.

"I am here for you," Ms. V continued. "I will pray with you, sit with you and continue to love you for the beautiful woman you are. Who do you think Myra has?"

Her question seemed to get Madison's attention, and she let out a silent relieved breath.

Her friend began to quickly blink back her tears and gave her a warm smile.

"You're right," Madison acquiesced, as she rubbed her head. "I allowed my hurt to get the better of me. She's just so rude and angry and...rude. Weren't you bothered by that, Beatrice?"

"Sure," Ms. V said. "But anger will usually only fuel anger. Our job, our great commission, is to share the Gospel; not just in word, but in deed. One of the ways to open a door to sharing the Gospel is kindness. Kindness goes a long way, Madison."

Madison nodded her agreement. "When I grow up, I want to be just like you."

Ms. V. tried unsuccessfully to stifle the laugh that came to her throat. "Oh, honey. Don't aim so low."

There was a beat of silence before Madison spoke again. "So, are you going to eat that?" Ms. V. followed her friend's gaze to her Jell-O.

Ms. V. shook her head and chuckled as she pushed the small container over to Madison, who took it gratefully and opened it immediately.

"Mmm. Strawberry," Madison said before tipping the container up to her lips.

Ms. V. didn't even try to stifle the laugh that came to her lips.

The noise level and undercurrent of the teacher's lounge returned to its normal state of relaxation and joviality. Ms. V. wouldn't be surprised if Myra's appearance would be marked as a cornerstone to the lunch hour, and the staff would later refer to their conversations in terms of B.M. and A.M., for Before Myra and After Myra.

Ms. V. took one last glance around the room, amazed at the staff's ability to shrug off the interruption. It was as if they took control of the rest of the time they had for lunch. Obviously, they knew how precious these moments to themselves were. Ms. V. prayed many days and weeks would go by before another incident interrupted the teacher's lunchtime. For many of them, it was the only peace they received all day, and she could tell by their actions that they were thankful for those quiet moments.

Chapter 5

The Lord hath appeared of old unto me, saying, Yea, I have loved thee with an everlasting love: therefore with lovingkindness have I drawn thee.
Jeremiah 31:3

"He loves unconditionally."

Ms. V. hated the feeling of being late. The angst and anxiety associated with running behind bothered her so much that she did whatever possible to keep it from happening. This morning, however, being late seemed unavoidable. It didn't matter that she sped up her movements so she could complete her morning rituals quicker, or that she skipped making her morning breakfast shake. She couldn't regain the few moments she took before getting out of bed.

A couple of minutes weren't worth the angst and worry of missing an important appointment, but without them, she wasn't sure she would have been able to make it that morning.

The middle of the week had never affected her energy this much. She decided to bypass the administrative office so that she could call her doctor's office before her first session that morning.

***

Ms. V. checked her desk calendar and counted the days between the present and the one…two…two and a half weeks it would take before she could get in to see her doctor. She knew she shouldn't have waited so long, but it was hard to break the habits she'd made when she had more energy. She'd been hoping the fatigue would have passed with a few good night's rest and a diet heavy in fruits and vegetables, but she finally had to relent. Now she prayed she hadn't waited too long, and that God would have mercy on her and her body until she could get in to see her doctor in eighteen days.

***

Ms. V. sat at her desk, dealing with the ever-growing pile of paperwork. She sifted through the files, feeling as though she were forgetting something or someone. She struggled to stay focused on her task and finally set aside thoughts of her health challenges forced herself to concentrate on her work.

She continued to finger through the files until the name she'd been searching for jumped out at her.

Samantha Royce.

Ms. V. pushed the pile of folders and paperwork to the edge of her desk to give herself room and opened Samantha Royce's folder. Samantha was in her sophomore year at the Christian Academy. She'd been enrolled in Center of Hope since her freshman year, and was a very quiet girl. Her father was the pastor of New Bethel North Community Baptist Church on the north side of town. Ms. V. had heard of it, and of the services they provided to the underserved residents in that community. If she remembered correctly, after doing her annual spring cleaning a few years ago she'd donated some clothing to their drive. It was a thriving church. From what she could tell from the little interaction she'd had with teachers who attended their services, the members were an almost equal mixture of ages.

The last time she'd seen Samantha, the teen's appearance had changed, and so had some of her mannerisms. The changes weren't glaringly obvious, but Ms. V. was good at seeing what most people didn't want anyone else to see.

Samantha had caught her attention almost a month ago as she walked down the hall between classes with a couple of fellow students. Ms. V. was sure her father didn't know she congregated with the questionable pair.

It was part of the staff's job to help guide the youth and assist in shaping their focus. The teachers were there not only to educate students in subjects that would help advance them towards being productive adults, but to reinforce life lessons. It was every teacher's hope that the parents were molding their teens into trustworthy, responsible, God-fearing youth that would grow to be compassionate, honorable adults who didn't wish to grieve God.

Sometimes the parents left most of the teaching of these characteristics to the Christian Academy's faculty, doing the young person a great injustice.

Ms. V.'s heart went out to those students. She tended to observe them more than other students while seeking God's guidance on how to reach them before they came to her with a crisis. She had a feeling from what she'd witnessed in Samantha's demeanor recently, the girl might need to talk. That was the reason Ms. V. had scheduled a session with Samantha during first period.

Ms. V. glanced at the clock. She had a few minutes to go over Samantha's file before she arrived.

As Ms. V. scanned the dividers indicating the separate years in Samantha's folder, she noticed the differences between Samantha's freshman and her Sophomore year school pictures.

The changes were none too subtle. The open and hopeful look in Samantha's eyes had turned guarded and solemn. Ms. V. wondered what had put that distrust in the girl's gaze. She could guess by the changes in her hairstyle and lack of accessories even allowed by the Christian Academy to accompany the uniforms, but Ms. V. didn't lean on guesses. She trusted the discernment the Lord gave her and the way she was often led to pray.

She read through the notes and grades in Samantha's file, noticing the gradual decline in her grade point average and participation in extracurricular activities. Whatever was troubling Samantha was affecting her academic and personal life.

The soft knock on the door pulled Ms. V's attention away from the paper she was reading. She was about to get up to open the door, but the knock came again, and the door opened to reveal the student she'd been reading about.

That was odd. She was sure she'd locked her door when she'd come in that morning. She shrugged it off as she took in Samantha's appearance.

She could be forgiven for mistaking Samantha for a boy if she'd seen her walking down the street. The girl was clad in the uniform khaki slacks, but they were worn a couple of sizes too big, with a button-down shirt and sweater similar to the ones most of the male students wore. It was also two sizes too large.

"Hello Samantha," Ms. V. said. "Come sit down." She gestured to the chair in front of her desk.

She watched as the teen moved forward slowly and sat down without making eye contact with her.

Maybe she'd waited too long to have this session. She watched in silence as Samantha pressed her fingertips together, crossed them, then wrung them together, and still the teen didn't look up at her.

"Samantha?" Ms. V. finally prompted, and the girl met her gaze for a couple of seconds before returning her eyes to her lap.

Ms. V's curiosity turned to concern, and she again sought the Holy Spirit's guidance. What she received in her spirit was that of a wounded being. She wasn't sure if it was physical, mental, or spiritual, but the girl before her had withdrawn into herself so much it could take half a session just to get her to come out of her shell. Ms. V. decided to start from scratch and use her technique for breaking the ice, or just making students feel more comfortable.

"It's been a moment since I've had you in here, Samantha. Is that the name you still prefer?" Ms. V. asked.

"Sam." The girl responded quietly.

Ms. V. nodded before she continued. "I requested this session so we could get reacquainted. How has this school year been for you?"

The file had shown Ms. V. a great deal, but it was her job to find out what was causing the deterioration in Sam's grades. It was true that she had requested the session out of curiosity, but she knew it was only a matter of time before Administration scheduled an appointment between herself and Ms. Royce due to the decline in her academic performance.

When she received a shrug as an answer from Samantha, Ms. V. knew she would have to change directions.

"The last time we met you were taking piano lessons after school. Are you still taking them?" Samantha took a deep breath, letting it out slowly as she nodded.

"You seemed more enthusiastic about it then, too," Ms. V. said, hoping to pull the teen into the conversation.

"It was more fun when I had a goal," Samantha said, her voice full of sadness.

"Did you reach your goal?" Ms. V. asked

Samantha crossed her arms. "It's more like the goal was moved out of reach."

"How so?"

Samantha heaved a sigh. "I was taking lessons so I could play during services at church."

Ms. V. waited for her to continue. When she didn't, Ms. V. got up and came around her desk so she could sit across from the girl. She hoped the closer physical proximity would help bridge the chasm between them.

"Did that change?"

"Yes."

"I'm going to need a little more detail if I'm to understand why the change in this goal bothers you," Ms. V. said leaning forward.

"I was told that I can't play during Sunday services," Sam said seeming to get tired of their back and forth banter.

"Why?" Ms. V. asked

"My attire and behavior no longer positively represent the message my father's church is trying to send to its young members," Sam stated, in a monotone.

It was obvious she was repeating an adult's opinion, and from the barely-leashed sarcasm Ms. V. detected, she would guess the words came from someone in authority.

"Who told you this?"

"My father."

"And why do you think he said this to you?" Ms. V. asked

"He says I dress like a boy," Sam stated.

Ms. V. had to admit that she'd thought the same, but they would come back to that.

"Do you still want to play during Sunday service?" She asked.

Samantha shrugged.

"I'm going to need more than a shrug."

"Yes, but I don't want to if I have to wear a dress," Sam said wryly.

"Why?"

"Because I don't believe I need to wear a dress to worship the Lord." Sam said indignantly.

"Why do you think your father wants you to dress a certain way when you are in front of his membership?"

Sam shrugged again. "I don't know. Tradition?"

"It could be." Ms. V. conceded. "But it could also be that people get distracted by your attire and that makes it harder to usher them into worship."

"But that's not my fault if they're looking at me instead of praising and worshiping God," Sam said with a pout.

"Well, yes and no. In a world of perfect people, when everyone comes together to fellowship and worship, they approach the sanctuary with one purpose, in one accord. But people are not perfect, and they come to church for several reasons." Ms. V. watched Sam for a change in her expression but there was nothing.

"I'm sure your father hopes members of the congregation are mature in their relationship with Christ to the degree that attending church becomes an extension of their desire to gather together to praise and worship God. That is not always the case. They have trouble letting go of what is going on in their lives and are easily distracted. In the end, your choice of clothing may be what keeps them distracted just long enough to hinder them from reaching that place of praise and worship they've been called to." Ms. V. gave Sam a moment to think about that before continuing.

"Let's go deeper. Why has your clothing preference changed?"

"It represents how I feel and how I want to be seen."

Ms. V. didn't miss the use of the word 'represents,' or the tone Sam used as she spoke. There was a great deal of animosity coming off her at the moment, and Ms. V. knew that, though her questions might have brought them to the surface, the anger wasn't directed towards her.

"You told me your father believes you dress like a boy. Do you wish to be seen as a boy?"

Ms. V. watched as several emotions crossed the girl's features; surprise morphed into discomfort, which led to sadness, then resignation.

"Maybe," Sam said.

Ms. V.'s heart squeezed at the hurt in that one word. This girl was in so much pain. Much more pain than what could be addressed in their hour-long session.

"Is this one of the reasons why your participation in class has dropped?"

Sam went back to shrugging, but at Ms. V's look she obviously thought better of it.

"I figure if my father can go back on his promise, I can go back on mine."

"What was the promise?"

"He said if my extra practicing time on the piano didn't affect my grades or attendance, then once I was experienced enough to play for service, I could." The anger came forward in Sam's eyes.

"I worked hard in school. I participated in the extra-curricular activities my father chose for me. I received nothing less than a B for two years and because my father didn't like how I dressed he went back on his end of the deal."

Ms. V. took a deep breath. She had suggested student/parent sessions before, and this situation seemed like a good fit for that strategy since it looked like the problems Sam was willing to talk about centered around her father.

"Do you want to discuss why you feel more comfortable in your current attire?" Ms. V. asked inclining her head towards Sam's sweater.

"Not now, but can I come back?" Sam asked.

"Most definitely," Ms. V. said before pausing. "Would you consider expending a little more effort in your classes? Your grade point average is dangerously low. You are at the point where it could affect your ability to be promoted into the next grade."

Sam's eyes widened before she winced. "I didn't mean for it to get this bad. I just... I just wanted my father to know that our agreement couldn't just be thrown away."

"But in the process, you may be throwing away your academic future. Is your ability to get into a good college and expand your potential, worth giving up to prove a point to your father?"

Sam seemed to think about her question before she sighed and slumped in her chair. "It's not fair."

"Life rarely is, but with God's favor, it balances out pretty good."

"You really believe in God, don't you," Sam said more as an observation.

Ms. V. pressed her lips together for a moment to keep from smiling. The girl was serious, and she would treat her statement the same way.

"Yes, I do," Ms. V. stated emphatically. "He is my constant companion. He leads and guides me when I'm not sure which way to go or what decision to make. He gives me an understanding that brings me peace. What about you?"

"God is there. Sometimes I feel Him more than others. Like when I'm playing the piano or singing. I feel Him the most then. He talks to me and tells me how beautiful I am to Him. Sometimes I go to the church after school on days when I know there's nothing scheduled, and I play. His presence always makes me feel better. It's as if all of the things other people see wrong in me don't matter." Sam looked at Ms. V as she said the last.

Ms. V. kept her face blank, knowing they were entering sensitive territory.

"He loves unconditionally," Ms. V. said, then paused, knowing the silence was thick with the tension of what she hadn't said. He also has a heart that we can break." Ms. V. continued. "We tend to forget that when we are looking to be loved. I know I am guilty of taking Him for granted sometimes. Even at my age."

Sam's face fell and she went back to inspecting her hands.

"Would you like me to schedule a session for you and your parents? I will moderate to assist in the communication." Ms. V. offered the concession in order to keep Sam from withdrawing fully.

Sam looked up at her. "You would do that?"

"It's one of the reasons why I'm here," Ms. V. said. "My first service is to you and your wellbeing," she added honestly.

Sam's lips curved up slightly. It was the closest the teen had come to a smile since she'd stepped into the room. She nodded her a consent.

"Okay. I will make a note to schedule a parent and student session next week. Would you like to talk more right now?"

"No, not right now," Sam replied, sounding lighter.

"Could we come to an understanding regarding your schoolwork?" Ms. V. asked, not taking her eyes off of Sam.

"I will start doing my homework and participating in class again," Sam said, squirming in her seat a little.

"How far behind are you? Do you need a tutor?" Ms. V. asked the question in case part of the decline in Sam's grades was due to lack of understanding.

"No. I've attended most of my classes." She shrugged. "I just stopped turning in the work. I still understand what's going on."

Ms. V. shook her head. The girl was extremely intelligent. "So, you have the work?"

"Yes."

"Maybe you could ask your teachers if you could still turn them in. A grade representing a late assignment would still be better than no grade at all. Consider that."

"Do you think they will take them?" Samantha asked with a little more light in her eyes.

"It is definitely worth a try. You are very bright. Most students wouldn't be able to jump back in as you are proposing. Don't waste that gift."

Ms. V. watched as Sam swallowed before nodding, catching the emotion pooling in her eyes before she blinked it away.

"Let's close this session in prayer." Ms. V. suggested.

Sam nodded and bowed her head.

"Dear Heavenly, Father. I thank you for your daughter who you have given amazing gifts and talents," Ms. V. said, as a beginning of her prayer. She was then led to speak peace over the teen's heart, and that God soothed her emotions and bought clarity to her mind.

Ms. V. was prompted to speak encouraging words to the girl during the prayer and urged her to let her light shine amongst her peers. She asked God to continue to pour out His anointing upon Sam's hands and that she would lean on Him for all of her decisions. Ms. V. began to recite Proverbs 3:5 squeezing the child's hands occasionally as she was moved to do so. A sweet aroma filled the air around them and she could tell by the girl's breathing, which had slowed, that she was listening and receiving.

Before ending the prayer, Ms. V. asked God to help bind the family together as never before. She prayed that the confusion that had come in would be stifled and banished from their relationship. She prayed for God's peace and love to permeate Sam's home and surround her with a feeling of wellbeing. When she finished and looked at Sam. The girl's countenance was lighter, and she didn't seem as defeated.

Chapter 6

And if it seem evil unto you to serve the LORD*, choose you this day whom ye will serve*
Joshua 24:12

"Michael, Britney, Abe, Margaret, Sam, Patrick Jordan, Joel…"

Ms. V. ushered Sam out of her office and took advantage of the open hour to stop by the administrative office to collect her mail. She was hoping—no, expecting her prayers regarding Myra to be heard by God. Though the young woman was definitely hurting, she was working at a Christian Academy where there were moral standards and professional expectations. No teacher or staff member should have to gird themselves up before approaching Myra and her mercurial moods. Nevertheless, Ms. V. took a deep breath before pulling the door open to the office, determined to influence the atmosphere for the better rather than be affected by the woman's inability to control her emotions.

She spotted the medium-sized brown teddy bear attached to the larger-than-usual floral arrangement on the counter. The vibrant and cheery bouquet was full of lavender, blush-colored Cala lilies, blue larkspurs, and white daisies. She felt bad the instant the thought crossed her mind, but she almost hoped it wasn't for her. She didn't feel like being on the receiving end of yet another scoff or skeptical look from Myra, no matter how beautiful the flowers were.

She turned to the wall of mailboxes, which were no more than designated cubby holes. She collected the notes from her box and shuffled through them slowly before turning to see if there were any recent notes for calls that hadn't made it into her box.

When she finally turned toward the counter, she was surprised to find Myra leaning back in her chair staring at her.

"Good morning, Myra," Ms. V. said, using her friendliest voice.

"You have a recent death in the family?" Myra asked, startling Ms. V. into silence.

Ms. V. shook her head to the negative.

"Well, it's not your birthday," Myra said flippantly. "I checked."

The hairs on the back of Ms. V's neck stood on end. What was this woman going on about now?

"You don't look sick, and unless you have an admirer . . ." Myra's eyes roamed from Ms. V.'s high-bun hairstyle and passed her cross-cut blouse to the top of her skirt and back up. "Which I doubt, but who's to say." Myra waved a hand before standing and walking towards the vase of flowers and stuffed animal. "I just can't understand why you are receiving so much attention." Myra pushed the vase to the edge of the counter towards her, forcing Ms. V. to grab them or allow them to fall to the floor.

Heat rolled over Ms. V. at the woman's insolence, and try as she might, she couldn't quell the urge to respond.

"Well then, it is a good thing that your job does not require you to know *why* a person receives a package, just for you to hold onto it until they are able to retrieve it," Ms. V. said as straight-faced as possible.

"You don't have to get nasty about it. I was just curious is all." Myra sneered.

"No, Myra, curiosity is kindly making me aware that I have a package and asking me just as nicely who they are from, then waiting to see if I feel like sharing." She paused, staring at Myra for a beat or two before continuing. "Curiosity is not making assumptions about my personal life based on a few flowers delivered to my place of employment. Matter of fact, that reminds me more of a person that is envious of another person's good fortune."

"I'm not jealous," Myra protested hotly, sending her a scathing look. "What do I have to be jealous of you for?"

"I'm wondering the same thing." Ms. V. cut in. "You call it curiosity, but your attitude says something different." Ms. V. raised her hand when Myra opened her mouth. "I'm simply stating the vibe I'm getting from you. I don't know what I've done to cause you to be skeptical of any gifts I receive instead of just being happy for me. If you got flowers, I would be happy for you." Ms. V. said blinking at Myra, who shut her mouth and blinked back.

Myra turned back to her desk. "Go, take your flowers before the petals start falling all over my counter and I have to clean them up." She sat back at her desk, clicking her mouse.

Ms. V. took one more deep breath, hesitant about calling any more attention to herself. Unfortunately, if she'd gotten any recent messages, she'd need them.

"Are there any messages that have come in for me that haven't made it into my box yet?" She made her expression as benign as possible, disgusted that she had to cater to the other woman's insecurities.

Myra turned around quickly, defiance clearly written on her face, but she must have considered Ms. V's expression nonthreatening. She turned back to a small pile next to the phone. She sifted through them and got up to bring her two of the pink slips of paper without a word.

"Thank you," Ms. V. said, but Myra just sat back down and turned to face her computer again.

Ms. V. took a deep breath as she shifted the vase to a more comfortable position in the crook of her arm.

That was a bust. She thought as she walked back down the hall to her room. Myra was out of hand. Ms. V. knew deep down that Myra's attitude towards her wasn't personal, but her anger and unhappiness with her situation was now making it hard for her to be civil to the staff, let alone respectful. Ms. V. would continue to pray, but if things didn't change in a week or two, she would have to go to the principal.

***

Ms. V. breathed in deeply, allowing the tension from the day to seep from her muscles and back as she lay in bed. Her mind was more active than usual, and it was taking longer than normal to get to sleep. She admitted that she was still slightly troubled by the different things that happened during her day, including her reaction to Myra. She asked for God's forgiveness and peace in that situation and the reassurance that the rest of her concerns from the day would be taken care of.

She began to recite her favorite Psalm. For many years Ms. V. considered the 139th book of Psalm as a love note to God's people. It soothed her to know that God thought so much of His children.

1 O Lord, thou hast searched me, and known me.

² Thou knowest my downsitting and mine uprising, thou understandest my thought afar off.

³ Thou compassest my path and my lying down, and art acquainted with all my ways.

⁴ For there is not a word in my tongue, but, lo, O LORD, thou knowest it altogether.

⁵ Thou hast beset me behind and before, and laid thine hand upon me.

⁶ Such knowledge is too wonderful for me; it is high, I cannot attain unto it.

⁷ Whither shall I go from thy spirit? or whither shall I flee from thy presence?

⁸ If I ascend up into heaven, thou art there: if I make my bed in hell, behold, thou art there…

She had barely reached the 20th verse when sleep's heavy arms enveloped her.

***

"Sam." The name seemed to be pulled out of her instead of her yelling it across the field voluntarily. Her spirit knew even before she saw the young girl run towards her. Sam wasn't consumed by the enemy on the other side. She wasn't lost, and the euphoria that came over Ms. V. with that thought galvanized her all the more.

The field Ms. V. stood on wasn't much different than the one before, except the row of people held behind the line of demons were at a precipice. She could see how their feet shifted, keeping them on the edge of what she knew in her spirit was a gaping abyss. Behind them there was nothing. It was hard to describe nothing, but still, it was there; dark, black and still. It seemed to be waiting for them to fall, move wrong or be scared into taking one more step back. The terror she felt coming from the other side was palpable.

"Michael. God calls you forward. The blood of Jesus is upon you and compels you to come out from among them. Britney, Robin, Abe, Margaret." She yelled, only giving voice to her spirit that had taken control. "The blood of Jesus is upon you. Jesus intercedes for you. Don't deny His call. Don't deny His gift.

"Demon of anger and strife, I rebuke you in the name of Jesus. Demon of bitterness, I rebuke you in the name of Jesus. Demon of fear, I call you out and rebuke you in the name of Jesus. Let them go!" Ms. V. felt as though her body were a conduit being used to breathe life into the promptings of the Holy Spirit as He gave authority to her spirit to release the binds holding the children to the other side of the field.

Unlike the dream from the other night, she was both watching and participating. Her mind was on the sidelines while her body and voice were being used to rescue the beings on the other side.

Sam came close enough for her to reach, and she held her hand out far enough to connect with the girl's fingers as she ran by. The light that suffused the girl was blinding, and Ms. V. had to look away. It wasn't only bright, it was warm, and it removed the chill from Ms. V.'s body long enough for her to realize that she had been freezing.

Another child broke away from the chain of children and what looked to be adults from the other side. Ms. V. was surprised to see more people that she knew. She wanted to call to them, but when she opened her mouth someone else's name came from her lips.

Michael ran towards her and touched her shoulder at the last second as he ran by her. He, too, became consumed in bright light. She glanced back at the field to see Margaret, Robin and Abe running towards her.

Where was Britney? She scanned the field and saw that the child had gotten stuck in muck halfway across the field. The girl looked back over her shoulder at the line of people bound by demonic forces on the other side and sank into the ground. She turned back toward Ms. V., the indecision in her eyes cluing Ms. V. into what was going on.

"You have to make a decision. You can't serve two masters. Jesus loves you. He died for you. He wants to be with you forever, but He won't force you. Who do you want to be with?" She saw the girl look down at the ground continuing to give away at her feet. "Please!" Ms. V.'s voice rang out. God loves you. Jesus loves you." Ms. V. felt compelled to yell, watching the child struggle and feeling desperate. "I love you."

She watched the child look up at those words. Her face softened, then became taut with determination as she pulled herself out of the muck and mire and began running; first slowly, then faster until she was in a full outrun.

Robin, Abe, and Margaret ran past Ms. V., each reaching out to touch her, each being consumed from the inside out by the brilliant light.

She felt weak, as if the children had somehow drained her with each touch. Her body shook with fatigue, but she wasn't ready to give up. There were dozens of people still lined up on the other side.

"Jordan, Joel, Patrick." Her body jerked with the power of the shout that came from her. She widened her stance to steady herself against the wind that came from behind her, cooling her body even more. Her fingers felt like icicles and she flexed them to keep the circulation moving.

Ms. V. wanted to know what was behind her; where the people were going once they passed her, but she was prevented from turning, both by the wind and the fact that her body wasn't listening to her.

"The blood of Jesus was shed for you." Her voice was raw, but she kept screaming the words the Holy Spirit compelled her to utter. She watched as the people whose names she called disengaged from the line and began running towards her side of the field.

A mere breath later, Britney appeared in front of her not slowing or moving to the right or left. Britney came at her full force, not giving her a chance to move even if she could. The girl fell into her. She felt her soul shudder under the strain of Britney's hold. Even as Britney started to glow, she began to feel herself floating away. She didn't have the strength to stay in her body anymore.

At the very last second Britney let go and moved on and so did her heat, leaving Ms. V. enveloped in a cold so deep she didn't know how her blood was moving in her veins. She saw Jordan, Joel, and Patrick racing towards her with their hands outstretched. She didn't know if she could survive another touch, but she stood rooted to the same spot and closed her eyes.

God, please I need your strength. I need your healing. I need your touch if I'm to go on.

Ms. V. felt some of the cold recede from her innermost being, and warmth began to spread throughout the rest of her body. Jordan was almost upon her by the time the heat had reached the ends of her limbs and then her toes. Jordan touched her arm and Ms. V.'s breath caught then erupted from her lungs. She tried to hold on long enough for Joel and Patrick to reach her, but the floating sensation came back, pulling her away from her post. She reached out a hand but watched herself fade from the field as the two reached her side.

A heavy weight took hold of her middle, slamming her forcefully against the mattress of her bed, waking Ms. V. with a jolt. Her hand was outstretched, fingers reaching for something that was no longer there. As consciousness replaced sleep the sensation of being outside of her body lessened until she was sure it was her imagination.

What had she eaten the night before, and why was she so cold?

Her body trembled violently, and it seemed to take supernatural strength to slip out of bed so she could kneel.

***

Ms. V. moved around the kitchen with the grace and speed of a snail. She seemed to be wading through oil with each step. She glanced at the kitchen clock to see if it had taken as much time to get ready as she felt it did. Ms. V. was astonished to find that she was ahead of schedule, so she didn't try to rush through preparing breakfast or lunch. It felt good to relax while making the preparations for once.

She was having a hard time shaking the feeling that her dream had something to do with her fatigue and...lack of energy? It was more than energy that she was missing. It was deeper. It was as if she went to sleep and woke up with her virtue gauge on deficient.

Moving back and forth between the counter and refrigerator, Ms. V. gave in to the temptation to go over a few of the counseling sessions she knew were scheduled for that day. She normally tried to avoid taking the situations home - which meant spending her nights trying to work out counseling problems in her head and researching ways to help solve some of the student's issues with outside sources. Not at all healthy. She had been successful until recently. Right now, she couldn't help pondering over Porcha's struggles with her faith and how that impacted every other decision she was making. Ms. V. had prayed for the young woman each time she came to her spirit and hoped that their discussion had stuck with Porcha and she applied some of the guidance they'd gone over.

Ms. V. considered Porcha's situation all the way to her car, praying for her most of the way.

It wasn't until Ms. V. drove onto the parking lot of the school that she felt a calm come over her. This was the place where she made a huge difference. Though the scenario might change daily due to the people she interacted with and what they were going through, she knew these people – well, most of them- which kept the possibilities within a range she was comfortable with.

Ms. V. took measured steps to the administrator's office. When she walked through the door and found Myra's chair empty, she breathed a sigh of relief. Though Myra's behavior struck her more like that of an insolent child looking for attention than something malicious, Ms. V. wasn't in the mood for any of Myra's snide remarks or attitude, if she were honest. Ms. V. felt slightly convicted by her thoughts. She shouldn't be so happy Myra wasn't at her post. Maybe the woman bothered her more than she told herself. She just needed a few minutes of quiet and prayer time for herself in her office before the first counseling session began.

Ms. V. went to her mail cubbyhole and removed a few sheets of paper, which were more than likely memorandums and smaller slips that held messages. Then her hand landed on a small, but thick envelope. It wasn't shaped like most of the school's correspondence, causing her to look at it more closely. It was only addressed Ms. V.

She began unsealing the envelope as she exited the office. The last thing she needed was for Myra to walk in and see her with yet another piece of correspondence that had nothing to do with administrative work.

Ms. V. was halfway down the hall, headed toward her office before she got the envelope open. There was a card inside it, and she pulled it out. She moved closer to the edge of the hallway to get out of the way of any passersby as she slowed to get a better look at the front of the card. It was exquisite. That was the only word that came to mind as she took in the pearlized, rose-colored cover with embossed silver orchids. The words, written in intricate calligraphy, read, *"You are in our thoughts."*

She opened the card to see just whose thoughts she was in and her breath caught. There had to be at least ten signatures on the left inside page and just as many on the right, surrounding the pre-typed message, which read, *"It's hard not to consider praying for a person as kind and generous as you. You are appreciated, not just for all you do, but the extra mile and smile you give to everyone."*

Ms. V. stopped short and leaned again the wall just a few steps from her office door. She was overwhelmed by the thoughtfulness of the former and current students and staff who sent her the card. It might be one thing if she were noticeably sick or hospitalized, but here she was, going about her job of listening to people and the Holy Spirit so she could give out the most beneficial advice, and someone thought enough of her to coordinate such a beautiful gesture.

Ms. V. disengaged from the wall, her throat beginning to burn with the effort it took to keep the tears at bay. Hopefully, she could stave them off until she reached the safety of her office. She was so grateful to work at this academy. No matter what came her way today, or the rest of the week, for that matter, this card made it all worth it.

Chapter 7

Trust in the LORD with all thine heart; and lean not unto thine own understanding.
Proverbs 3:5

"Trust not in man but God."

Ms. V. was so engrossed in her thoughts, she didn't notice the man waiting by her door until she reached forward to unlock it. Glancing up, she nearly jumped out of her skin when her eyes met those of Mr. Sanderson.

Ms. V.'s hand went up involuntarily over her blouse-covered chest. "Mr. Sanderson. I didn't see you there." Mr. Sanderson's brown eyes widened then softened with contrition. "I'm sorry. I didn't mean to startle you," he said, sliding his hands into the pockets of his dark brown slacks.

Mr. Sanderson, Center of Hope's head science teacher, looked to be in his early forties, if the light sprinkling of gray at his temples was any indication. But for all Ms. V. knew, he could have been in his fifties. His hazelnut-hue hid any small lines at the edges of his almond-shaped eyes. The rest of his facial features, including his wide nose and thin lips made him a pleasant looking man. In all, he was just above average-looking. His face was kind, and she could tell that he kept active because his six-foot physique was more athletic than thin. He'd always struck her as a loner, so her surprise was due to both finding someone at her door, and that someone being him.

Ms. V. waved away his apology. "No. It was all me. I wasn't paying attention to my surroundings." She took a deep breath to calm her racing heart. "How are you doing this morning?"

He hesitated for a moment and shifted from one foot to another. He ran his thumb across his forehead as she'd seen him do when he was working through a problem. "Um, yeah, good, good. I was wondering if I could talk to you for a moment." Unease radiated from him.

Ms. V. blinked at him once in surprise then burst into action. "Sure. Let me just get the door open and the lights turned on."

She opened the door but was met with a room bathed in light. It stopped her in her tracks, causing Mr. Sanderson to bump into her. She pitched forward, sure the floor would rush up to meet her, but strong hands caught her upper arms, stopping her forward motion.

She murmured another apology, too preoccupied by her near stumble and the illumination of the room. She always turned her lights off.

"What's the problem?" Mr. Sanderson asked even as he stepped around Ms. V.

"The lights are on," Ms. V said. "I never leave my lights on." She scanned the space without advancing any further into the room.

"May I take a look?" Mr. Sanderson asked.

"Sure. Sure, thank you." Ms. V. replied, then watched him make a B-line for the standing screen in the corner of the room, then to her desk, which he looked under before coming back her way.

"Did you have a maintenance order in? I know they've been behind. Is there a chance you put one in so long ago you forgot?"

Ms. V. tried to think back, but kept coming up short. She couldn't seem to remember anything beyond the last two weeks. Had her life really been so routine that she couldn't distinguish one day from another? She took a deep breath to calm herself before she answered.

"I don't recall. It's as if I was just dropped into this week. I say that to mean, I remember yesterday and Monday, but if I try to remember anything in particular from two weeks ago it just looks a lot like yesterday and Monday. Either that, or it's blank, but that wouldn't make sense." She walked over to her desk to put her purse and other belongings down and rubbed her right temple.

"I notice that you've been looking a little under the weather lately," Mr. Sanderson said. Have you seen a doctor?" He stood in the middle of her room, glancing around every now and then as if he may have overlooked a hiding place.

She followed his gaze the first two times but soon realized he was standing in the middle of her room because she hadn't invited him to sit down.

"Please forgive me. Would you like to sit here, or over there?" She gestured between the two chairs in front of her desk and her less formal area.

She watched him scan the chairs next to her then turn to look at the sitting area behind him.

"The sitting area would be fine."

"Okay." She swept her arm out, gesturing for him to go to the sitting area while she checked her desk to see if anything had been disturbed, took off her jacket, and stowed her purse in the drawer.

She glanced at the clock on the way to the sitting area. She didn't have anyone scheduled during the first period, but she thought Mr. Sanderson had a class. She did a double-take when she realized that classes weren't to begin for another half an hour. Had she really left her home that early? Did she miss the changing of the time? No. That wouldn't explain it. Maybe she spent more time in the administrative office being pestered every morning by Myra than she realized.

Ms. V. sat down on the couch, opposite to Mr. Sanderson, who sat in one of the chairs. His legs were crossed at the knee, but he sat too rigidly to be relaxed.

"Okay, Mr. Sanderson, what can I do for you?" She looked him square in the eye while she smoothed her long skirt with her palms.

He took a moment as if he were trying to organize his thoughts. Then he cleared his throat and began. "From our previous conversations, I know you to be a woman of God, a woman of faith. I'm in need of some guidance and I was hoping you could help me. I've been struggling with a decision and I need some advice."

Ms. V. was surprised at the man's openness. She wondered if he'd been wrestling with this decision for a long time, or if he was used to being this straightforward with his feelings?

"Sure. I will do whatever I can." She answered with all sincerity, even if she was not yet sure she could help.

Mr. Sanderson took a breath as he glanced down for a moment. His eyes, hidden by his lids, moved back and forth as if he were tracing a pattern in the floor.

He looked up at Ms. V. just before he opened his mouth. "It's my sister Margaret." He let out another breath as if getting up the courage to form the next words. "She has been diagnosed with non-Hodgkins lymphoma." Ms. V. watched him uncross his legs and shift forward slightly in his chair. "Margaret lives in Michigan. She moved there with her husband seven years ago. He was diagnosed with early-onset Alzheimer's a year ago."

Ms. V. let out a silent breath of her own. There was a great deal of suffering in that family, but instead of reconfirming that with him, Ms. V. simply nodded for him to continue. Mr. Sanderson's shoulders visibly relaxed, as if her small non-verbal instruction gave him the permission he needed to finish opening the flood gates.

"Margaret and I are pretty close. We don't have any other siblings, and our parents died when I was in my late twenties. Margaret is three years older than I am, and a very private person, but we've always had a good friendship." Mr. Sanderson moved to the edge of his chair, his eyes growing intense.

"That's why I was hurt when my brother-in-law called me during one of his more lucid moments a month ago and told me about her illness. She is currently undergoing an aggressive type of chemotherapy that, from his words, makes her sick from sunup to sundown."

Mr. Sanderson stood up and began to pace as if his body were no longer able to contain the emotions from his sitting position. Ms. V. followed him with her eyes and began praying that God would pour out His peace upon Mr. Sanderson and his situation. She also prayed for understanding regarding their talk and that Mr. Sanderson truly have an ear to hear what God wanted him to know. She'd failed to pray them into the conversation, but it didn't mean she couldn't still cover the entire conversation from here on with prayer.

"Peter, Margaret's husband, asked me for help. They have a nurse that comes in for a few hours a day, but her specialty is dealing with the elderly or those struggling with dementia or Alzheimer's. Though some of the care she provides can be shared, they are only insured to use her for his needs during the hours she has already been scheduled. Peter said Margaret is also considering alternative treatment, which means they will have to refinance, but if I sell my home and take a sabbatical it would solve most of the financial burdens and care issues."

"What did your sister say?" Ms. V. asked, using her voice to help soothe him so he would be able to answer her question.

He glanced at her and stopped pacing. "One more thing about my sister is that she's stubborn and prideful. I called her the next day, and she tried to deny it at first, saying Peter was paranoid due to his illness."

"Did he sound paranoid?" Ms. V. asked, both out of curiosity and to help him work through his thoughts.

"No, but knowing my sister, I figured I would need more than Peter's word when I spoke to her. While I was on the phone with him the day before, I asked him to take pictures with his phone of any paperwork.

"With no way to deny it, she confirmed that what Peter told me was true, but that he had no right to burden me." Mr. Sanderson sat back down. "I was so angry with her. We were each all the other had between the time our parents died and the time she married Peter. For her to say that to me—well, it floored me, and then the anger set in. We argued, and she said she would call me later, but she hasn't." Mr. Sanderson's eyes became suspiciously moist, but she could tell the overflow of emotion stemmed from helplessness and frustration more than sadness or hopelessness.

She gave him a moment to get his emotions under control.

"I put in for Family Emergency leave and went to see them. Peter was right. Her reaction to the chemotherapy was wearing her down and she still had three more sessions. She was considering giving up chemo for the alternative treatment, but I convinced her to wait until the chemo cycle was done and she received her results." He stopped speaking and look at Ms. V., who nodded in agreement.

"That makes sense," she responded.

"Yeah. So, I paid for another caregiver just until she got through the chemo. She ranted and raved, but I convinced her that I would stay if she didn't accept the help." He ran his hands over his close-cropped hair in frustration.

"Okay. It sounds like you've been getting through to her. I'm sure she appreciates everything, even though she may not be able to tell you."

"I know. It was an exercise in frustration those first few weeks, but I'm glad I went. I think more than anything, she felt like she was on her own. I looked up some support groups and drove her to a couple. Leaving was still painful, but bearable." He rubbed his forehead. "You know, I don't believe my relationship with God has ever been stronger. It has taken a great deal of prayer to work through my parents' deaths and Peter's illness. My sister has lost so much…" He stopped as if he were struggling with himself. Ms. V. just observed. It looked like he needed an ear more than the advice he requested.

"I asked God what I should do, but I'm not sure if my emotions are overriding what He's saying," he said, more to himself than her. "I've had my eye on the principal's position here."

Ms. V. must not have hidden her shock well, because after one glance he stopped the direction of his dialogue.

"No, Principal Wake has not said anything about retiring or moving on, but he's getting older and we've talked. He knows I'm interested and has even given me advice. I know what it takes to be considered, but I'm at an impasse after the report my sister received last week." He rubbed his slacks above his knees.

"I've been praying and so has my church, but more than that, each time I've gone to God on her behalf He has answered my supplication favorably and reiterated that she will heal," Mr. Sanderson said, but instead of looking elated, he seemed even more troubled.

"I'm struggling with what I see and what I know God has said. I'm afraid I've misunderstood His meaning and I will be left here alone. She's my last living family member, and it doesn't look like anything is working. Even more, it looks like things are going in the opposite direction. People have told me to continue to trust in the Lord and I am, but it is so hard not to allow fear to take hold."

Ms. V. was about to open her mouth to respond, but she was prompted to remain still and watch him sit across from her and struggle. He continued to stare at the floor, shaking his head as if trying to clear it from whatever thoughts had taken hold. When he finally looked up the tears were evident.

Ms. V. picked up the box of tissue from the side table next to the couch and placed it in front of him, keeping eye contact with him the whole time to avoid drawing his attention to what she was doing. She didn't want to do anything that would cause him to withdraw when he was so close to getting his answers.

Mr. Sanderson resumed his part of the conversation. "I'm afraid she's leaving information out. I don't trust her to tell me everything and I'm afraid she is suffering in vain. I want to go to her, but I have been told in no uncertain terms not to because she's afraid I will end up staying and throwing away my dream. I've told her I can start again, but I can't get another sister." He pulled a tissue from the box and swiping it across each eye.

Ms. V. waited to see if he would continue, but when he didn't, she checked her spirit and received her answer. "It would be good if you could get a straight answer from her, I'm sure, but your trust shouldn't lie with her. It should lie with God. He has answered you numerous times. It may be because He knows how stubborn your sister is or because He wants you to be a witness to someone, maybe even your sister. I'm glad for your sake that you have a personal relationship with God. This would be so much harder without it." She watched him for a moment, hoping to truly draw all of his attention before she shared her next thought.

"You have talked through a great deal," she continued. "And I hope you have been listening to yourself, because it sounded to me as though you've answered some of your own questions. God never told us that when we accepted Him in our hearts that we would feel no more pain, not go through any more trials, never lose another person close to us. He only promised that He would never forsake you, that He would draw you closer, give you peace and use you to advance the Kingdom of heaven. Listen to Him when He speaks peace upon you and tells you there is nothing to fear."

Ms. V. shifted on the couch as she shifted direction. "Did God tell you to let go of your job, sell your home and move to Michigan?"

He thought about her question for a moment. Then his shoulder's sagged and she received her answer before he even opened his mouth.

"No." He whispered.

"Then don't move," she replied. "If you move without absolute confidence in God's direction and give up your career and potential future to go take care of your sister, the enemy may get a foothold. It may be too easy to give in to thoughts of resentment. If you don't move and aren't sure you've heard God in that respect, you may have to deal with the guilt of not being there to help take care of your sister firsthand. But in either instance, if you have a clear answer from God, you will have peace and clarity on what to do next, not only for her, but for yourself." Ms. V. leaned back a little on the couch to relieve some of the tension in her back that had come with the intensity of her gaze and comment.

"Isn't family supposed to take care of one another though?" he asked, looking uncertain.

"Absolutely, and you have been, by visiting them, making sure both of them have home care, and ensuring she had people to talk to who were going through or had gone through what she is. That is huge, but I guess if you didn't think it helped to talk to someone with shared values, you wouldn't be talking to me."

"Point taken," Mr. Sanderson said before slowly exhaling. He glanced up at the clock. "Thank you, Ms. V. This time with you has helped me immensely."

"I'm glad to hear it." Ms. V. replied softly.

"Do you mind if I come back from time to time? I could make an appointment." He straightened the suit jacket he'd never taken off.

"An appointment would be good, even though you seem to know when I'm available." She gave him a small smile to soften her words.

He nodded his agreement. "Thank you Ms. V. Really."

"You're welcome," she replied, before putting up a hand to signal for him to stay.

"I failed to open up this conversation with a prayer, and though I prayed throughout our talk, I would like to close it out with prayer."

"Yes. Please. Thank you." Mr. Sanderson bowed his head.

She did the same before she began.

Dear Heavenly Father,

We come before your throne humbly, yet boldly, thanking you for giving us the desire to acknowledge You, to come to You with not only our praise but our supplications. You are the great 'I Am' and there is no one beside you. Father, I lift up my brother John Sanderson to you and his sister Margaret. I am asking for your peace that surpasses all understanding to rest on his shoulders. Please comfort him while your healing hand rests upon his sister, Margaret. You have given him your word that she will be healed. Please help John stand in that knowledge so that his mind will be clear to hear Your voice when You direct him on whether to go tend to his sister and brother-in-law or stay here. You have so many things you can do to help this situation and he wants to make sure he is in your perfect will as do I. Thank you for your love and your unfailing grace, mercy and faithfulness to us. We pray all of these things in the precious name of your son, Jesus Christ. Amen.

When she lifted her head and looked into his eyes, she saw a clarity that confirmed that her silent prayers during their talk had been answered. His mind had shifted and his relationship with God stood above all others. He was in line to hear and she was at peace.

"Thank you, Ms. V." Mr. Sanderson whispered.

"Your welcome," she replied. "God is so good. Isn't He?"

Mr. Sanderson nodded as he stood. "The best."

She smiled up at him. "See you at lunch."

He turned as he reached the door. "Yes. I hope it's relatively drama-free."

She shrugged, smiling. "One can only hope and pray, but I think we've started this day on such a wonderful note; how could it not get better?"

Mr. Sanderson smiled back before opening the door. "How, indeed," he said and was halfway through the door when she called out to him. "Blessings be upon you."

"Yes, and also you," he said with a chuckle before exiting.

Ms. V. inhaled deeply and leaned back on the couch. No Myra, and a day that started like this? She was blessed.

Chapter 8

Are not five sparrows sold for two farthings, and not one of them is forgotten before God? But even the very hairs of your head are all numbered. Fear not therefore: ye are of more value than many sparrows. Luke 12:6-7

"Keeping Kevin isn't worth losing your self-worth over."

Ms. V.'s eye popped open at the quiet knock on the door. Had she been asleep? She glanced around to find that she was still on the couch. *Oh no.* Her heart rate kicked up. She looked up at the clock and exhaled in relief. They were still in the first period. Thank goodness for whoever knocked on her door. No telling how long she would have slept. She had always tried to be careful not to allow the sounds of her aquarium to lull her to sleep, but instead, soothe her and be an accompaniment to her time of meditation. She glanced at the aquarium, noting the pieces of food still floating on top of the water, letting her know that she hadn't forgotten to feed them as she had the day before.

Ms. V. was halfway to the door when it opened and her friend Madison stuck her head in.

"Hey. Pssst. We're watching a film today so I thought I would peek in for a second to tell you that Myra isn't here today," her friend said with a mischievous grin. "How are you doing? I like that top. Anyway, I think some of the teachers are planning a potluck." Madison finished in a stage whisper.

Ms. V. laughed, glancing down at her blouse for a second. It took that long to catch up with Madison's shifting train of thought. "You're kidding. A potluck?"

"Nope. The word is spreading, so I thought I would give you a heads up so you can order something. If you want to." Madison added after a quick pause.

Ms. V. thought about it for a moment. It sounded like a fun idea. Too bad it was due to someone's absence instead of their presence. "Sure. I'll send out for some sandwiches. Or is there a list?"

"Nope, no list, it'll be whatever people can think up," Madison said with a bigger smile than Ms. V. had seen on her face in a while.

"Okay. Good. Thank you for letting me know."

"You're welcome. I'll come back just before lunch and we can walk over together."

"Okay." Ms. V. replied and shook her head after Madison closed her door. She walked to her desk and went to the small file folder of restaurants that delivered in case she forgot to prepare something for a preplanned potluck or birthday party. She placed the call, ordering a couple dozen half-sandwiches with a variety of fillings and bread options. Once she was assured that it would be delivered before the school's set lunchtime, she gave them her credit card number. She was looking forward to a nice peaceful lunch in the companionable silence of the teachers' lounge.

***

An hour and a half later there was another knock on the door. Ms. V. called out for the person to enter and watched as Porcha walked through the door and closed it slowly behind her. The young woman was as prompt as usual for their session.

From what Ms. V. remembered, the majority of their last session dealt with Porcha's relationship with Kevin, and her fear that God had distanced Himself from her. By the end of the counseling session, Ms. V. was sure that Porcha understood that the quietness Porcha had been experiencing in her relationship with God was His attempt by Him to draw her closer. The young woman had left with more confidence in her walk with God and more determination to remain celibate. This was also something Ms. V. lifted up to God in her prayers from time to time.

The Porcha she met with before did not resemble the young woman with the somber expression that stood before Ms. V. at this moment. She seemed to harbor an expectation of chastisement, and Ms. V.'s stomach dropped. She hoped the teen hadn't done anything that would set back her relationship with God. She knew it wasn't the act that separated people from God but the guilt that kept them from accepting God's forgiveness and love.

"Good morning, Porcha." Ms. V. greeted when the girl sat down.

"Morning, Ms. V." Porcha responded, her eyes meeting Ms. V.'s for the barest moment before skittering away.

"How are you?"

Porcha shrugged. "Not too good."

Ms. V. could have guessed that, but quietly waited while Porcha worked out what she wanted to say in her mind. Ms. V. breathed in and exhaled a silent prayer that Porcha would be comforted by God. She asked the Holy Spirit for the words and wisdom to guide the girl.

"I just wanted to tell you that you were right. I can't continue to put Kevin off and I shouldn't allow him to pressure me to do something I'm not ready to do even though I love him." The tears began and Porcha pulled a few sheets of tissue from the box sitting on the edge of the desk.

Ms. V. was pleasantly surprised by Porcha's admission but wondered what brought about this change in reasoning since the last time they spoke. Hopefully the peace Porcha had found in her understanding that God had not left her but was drawing her closer, had something to do with it.

"What changed your mind?" Ms. V. asked crossing her fingers in front of her. She watched Porcha's face crumple.

"Majestic is pregnant." Porcha blurted out. Ms. V. had to admit that she hadn't seen that coming.

"My best friend is pregnant. She's only sixteen. Sixteen, Ms. V." Porcha's hands moved frantically with her words. The girl was growing more distraught by the moment.

"Take a deep breath, sweetie. You don't want to make yourself sick." Ms. V. leaned forward in her chair.

Porcha took a deep breath visibly shivering and wiped her eyes.

Ms. V. waited for the child to compose herself before talking. "What about your friend's situation caused you to change your mind?" She asked.

Porcha looked up at her with her mouth hanging open. "She's pregnant." She said it as if that should have explained everything.

"Yes. You've told me, but what does her pregnancy have to do with your decision not to let Kevin pressure you into having premarital sex?"

Porcha's mouth opened and closed a couple of times, making her look like one of the fish in Ms. V.'s aquarium in the office

"I don't want to get pregnant. That would ruin my life." Porcha stated without sparing the dramatic eyeroll.

"Well, it would certainly be more challenging, but as per our conversation last week. But there are plenty of other consequences that can come from premarital sex."

Porcha humphed. "I know, but it's not like someone can look at you and tell you are no longer a virgin. And if I am feeling insecure about it, I can keep my mouth shut."

Ms. V. nodded to show that she was listening. "So, you are more afraid of what your friends and family will say if they know you are having sex than what *God* thinks of you fornicating. Not to mention, that you are taking the Holy Spirit along for the act since you were filled." Porcha blinked a few times at her, seeming at a loss so she backed up for a moment.

"They weren't the reasons we spoke of at the end of the session last week." Ms. V. noticed that although Porcha had looked up at her, she was no longer looking her in the eyes.

"Porcha?" She prompted when the girl continued to avoid her gaze.

"You mean the spiritual part?" Porcha said with some reluctance.

"I got the feeling last week you were more concerned about your relationship with God than you were with your relationship with Kevin. Is that no longer the case?"

Ms. V. watched her carefully, wondering what had happened during the week to make Porcha backpedal from her conviction on the subject. The girl had been clear in her desire to follow God's word regarding living by the spirit and not being controlled by the flesh.

"I know being intimate with Kevin is something I may not be ready for, even though he seems to be. But I know neither of us are ready for marriage, which is what we said we would wait for. I am just concerned at how impatient has he's been acting over the last two weeks." Porcha placed her hands over her face and took a deep breath. "I can't believe I'm about to say this."

Ms. V. leaned back in her chair to give the child space so she didn't think she was being pushed into her next confession.

"When I'm with him, with Kevin, he's so nice and he says such wonderful things" Porcha continued. "He's the smartest and cutest guy I know, and he picked me. We have so much fun together and I really feel like that he listens to me and knows what I'm going through. He gets me." Porcha shrugged. "He hasn't said those words, you know, the ones about loving me, but he's shown me in the way he is with me." Porcha looked up and Ms. V. almost pleading with her to understand.

Ms. V. let out a breath. "Honey, are you trying to talk me into giving you a pardon in this instance or are you trying to convince yourself that it is all right to have premarital sex?"

Porcha looked down at her hands and the silence stretched out between them

"I don't want to lose him."

And there they were. At the center of it all.

Since Porcha had finally been straightforward with her, she in turn would be straightforward with Porcha. "He isn't worth keeping if he can't respect your wish to remaining abstinent or your desire to get closer to God."

"I know, I know…" was all Porcha said before rubbing her forehead then temples with the heels of her hands.

"Keeping Kevin isn't worth losing your self-worth over. You are still the same sweet, bright and beautiful young woman you were when you made your vows of purity with your father. You are still the same very valuable young woman you were when you slipped on that ring." Ms. V. said after noticing how Porcha played with her purity ring.

"You weren't any less of those things when you entered into your relationship with Kevin. Don't let anything or anyone convince you otherwise. Keep hold of your identity and the value you saw in the mirror before Kevin. That young woman was what he saw first. Love the young woman you see there." Ms. V. paused until Porcha looked up from her hands.

"No one is worth compromising your identity for. Not even an intelligent, handsome, young man with all the right words who should like you enough to be happy that you want to wait."

"Happy? Ms. V. I don't know about happy." Porcha giggled.

"Well, maybe not happy, but honored to have a girl who keeps her word to God."

Dawning came into Porcha's eyes and though they were still solemn the conviction was back.

A determined look replaced the tears in Porcha's eyes, and she nodded and smiled wanly...

"I have to get to class," Porcha said, and Ms. V. looked up at the clock, startled at the quick passage of time.

"Isn't it about to be lunch period?"

"Yes, but I'm doing some extra credit for Ms. Alvarez's for Spanish."

Ms. V. nodded and smiled at Porcha. "Okay, then let's pray.

"Dear Lord, Keep your child, Porcha. Show her the beauty inside of her. Nurture in her a relationship of love with you and herself that will cultivate an understanding of how valuable she is. Teach her how to love herself and that she is worthy of such love. In Jesus' name. Amen.

Silently, Ms. V. prayed that their conversation would remain in Porcha's mind and heart longer than their last one and that the girl would receive an understanding of her worth and value that couldn't be measured by the amount of affection she received.

After Porcha left Ms. V. straightened her desk and personal items as she waited for Madison to meet her. She made a quick call to the office to make sure her sandwiches were not only delivered, but that one of the staff walked them down to the teacher's lounge.

When Stacey Richards answered the phone, Ms. V. smiled to herself in relief at not having to speak to Myra first. As the school's bookkeeper, Stacey usually kept to herself, choosing to eat her lunch at her desk, but she was a very sweet woman to talk to whenever she took over the phones.

Once Ms. V. had confirmed that her sandwich order had been delivered to the teacher's lounge, she thanked Stacey and considered again how pleasurable a call to the office could be.

Ms. V. said a quick prayer for Myra and whatever situation she was in that caused her to take a day off. She didn't give in to the temptation of praying for more days without Myra, but instead prayed for her physical and mental health.

She had just finished with Madison's swift knock came. Madison poked her head in. "You ready, Bea?" She didn't miss the gleam in her friend's eye and shook her finger at her.

"What?" Madison asked.

"You shouldn't be so quick to celebrate another person's bad fortune," Ms. V. said. "For all we know, Myra may have had a death in the family."

Madison's smiling features turned contrite. "You're right. I promise to eat my share of the potluck food in the drama free teacher's lounge with as little celebration as possible."

Ms. V. couldn't help the laugh that bubbled out of her at her friend's words. Madison was incorrigible. Ms. V. nodded and followed Madison out of the door.

Chapter 9

Praying always with all prayer and supplication in the Spirit, and watching thereunto with all perseverance and supplication for all saints. Ephesians 6:18

… Myra receive peace and healing for her pain.

There were no decorations, but the atmosphere in the teacher's lounge reminded Ms. V. of the end of the school year parties that the teachers' threw for themselves. The room was alight with activity and the sound from the conversations was just above a steady hum.

Ms. V. noted the smiles and lightness of everyone's countenance and thanked God for this reprieve. No doubt the students would be treated to a little more attentiveness and patience from their teachers in the classroom after lunch. It struck her that Myra's attitude had oppressed both the teachers and students alike.

Ms. V. and Madison joined a table where a couple of other teachers sat enjoying their meal. Their plates were full of a variety of foods. Most of it seemed delivered upon the announcement of the impromptu potluck. Ms. V.s' mouth watered at the sight of the veggie pizza and Korean short ribs. She stood up, but Madison beckoned her to remain seated.

"I'll get our plates," Madison said. "I will make sure I put some of everything on your plate. I think I know by now what you like and don't like."

Ms. V. conceded, content to watch the teachers move back and forth from their seats to the buffet on the counter. Every possible spot was filled, from the utensil organizer to the microwave. She spotted Mr. McNeely do a little two-step on his way to the utensil tray, pick up a spoon then do a full twirl before heading back to his seat with a stride that would rival that of even John Travolta in Saturday Night Fever. Ms. V. couldn't help but smile at his obvious enjoyment at being free to roam where he pleased, but she tried to stifle the giggle. She wouldn't have suspected that Mr. McNeely possessed any such moves.

Ms. V. glanced around and noticed that Mr. Neely's improvised dance started something. Soon most of the teachers were doing some type of little dance as they moved down the buffet line, and the moves became more pronounced when someone turned on their phone's music app. The upbeat jazz filled the room but didn't make conversation a struggle. The vibe was happy, carefree and relaxing.

Ms. V. joined in on the laughter from time to time when someone struck out, doing a full out move to a certain beat to a song. Funny thing; it was always in front of the microwave.

Ms. V's attention went back to Madison as her friend set a plate of food down in front of her.

The anticipation Ms. V. had felt at the thought of partaking of some of the foods she'd seen on the other two teacher's plates waned.

Ms. V. looked down at her plate then over to her friend's plate. She glanced up at Madison and raised a brow in question.

Madison shrugged. "I think we might have been late."

Ms. V. turned to look over at the counter that was almost overflowing with dishes only a minute ago. It was almost bare. *Huh.* "How could I not have at least gotten one of my own sandwiches?" Ms. V. asked out loud, though she was speaking more to herself.

Ms. V. took a closer look at her plate and frowned in confusion. There was what looked like garlic mashed potatoes, lime Jell-o, a fruit cup, peas and carrot squares and…She leaned in closer, was that apple sauce?

Miss V was tempted to push her plate away, except the smells of the room had started her mouth watering and she was hungry. She looked down at her plate one more time in disdain before forking up some potatoes.

It took a moment for Ms. V. to realize that a hush had come over the room. Someone had turned off the music, and a tension rolled through the lounge. Miss V looked up, following everyone's gaze to the doorway where a very puffy-eyed Myra stood.

The sound of an old needle running across a vinyl record came to Ms. V.'s mind as she considered the stillness of the room.

If it were possible, Myra looked hurt—no, wounded by the spontaneous party that was going on in the lounge. Then again, it didn't take an observant or terribly smart person to consider that the slowly drooping smiles and atmosphere in a room was due to their presence.

Ms. V. watched Myra stand there, not moving, but instead of her face morphing into an insolent frown, it crumpled, and the devastation that crossed her features pulled at Ms. V's heart.

She. got up as Myra's head dropped. The vulnerability and utter helplessness emanating from her was heartbreaking. Ms. V. was barely conscious of the people and chairs she moved around to reach Myra. By the time she stood in front of the young woman, Myra's head was so low Ms. V. was sure she had no clue who was standing in front of her, but when Ms. V. leaned forward, Myra cringed.

Ms. V. took a deep breath and wrapped her arms around the woman who had cost her so many smiles and moments of peace, but that wasn't what she was thinking about at that moment. All she thought about was that this woman was hurting, and she couldn't just let her stand there in her vulnerability and distress.

She hugged Myra tightly, beginning to pray quietly that Myra receive peace and healing for her pain. Ms. V. whispered softly into Myra's ear. "You are loved. Never forget that. You are valuable and you are loved."

Myra's body sagged as sobs began to rack her and Ms. V. began to struggle under the weight. Just when she thought her legs would give out from under her, she felt Myra's weight lift slightly. Simultaneously, she felt arms surround her from behind then from the side, each embrace relieving some of the stress of Myra's weight. It took Ms. V. a moment to realize what was happening, but when she did, her heart grew a few sizes in her chest, making breathing hard, especially around the lump forming in her throat.

Other teachers had gotten up from their seats and were now surrounding Myra both with their arms and prayers. Ms. V. was moved to tears. So, she cried along with Myra, surrounded by more than a dozen teachers who were praying and yes, also crying.

The only words needed were their prayers as they lifted Myra up.

A few minutes later, the teachers were able to get Myra to a chair at one of the nearby tables.

"Sorry I broke up your party," Myra said, sounding sincere.

"Pssh," Ms. V. said, smacking her lips. "We can party any time." It wasn't entirely true, but no one would have been able to tell by how quickly they pulled this little fiesta together. Although next time there should be a rule about taking seconds or thirds before everyone was able to partake.

Myra looked up at the crowd around her and blanched. Ms. V. glanced up as well.

"It's okay, everyone. You can go back to enjoying your lunch period. Myra and I will just sit right here and have a little chat." Ms. V. reached out and patted Myra's hand across the table for emphasis.

Most of the teachers shrugged but reached out to touch Myra's shoulder one by one as they left. Ms. V. looked up to see Madison still standing next to her. "It's okay." Ms. V. said to her friend, who looked reluctant to leave her alone.

"I'll be right over here, Bea," Madison said quietly, pointing at a neighboring table that gave Ms. V. and Myra enough privacy not to be overheard. Ms. V. was grateful for her friend's understanding and protection.

Myra dabbed her eyes with a tissue one of the other teachers handed her.

"Are you thirsty or hungry? Though I can only guarantee apple sauce at the moment."

Myra looked at Ms. V. oddly but shook her head in the negative.

"Do you want to talk about it?" Ms. V. asked and watched Myra begin to shrink into herself. "I'm just asking in case you wanted to, but I don't need you to in order to continue to pray for you," Ms. V. hastened to add.

Myra's shoulders relaxed. "Could I ask you a question?"

"Sure." Ms. V. Responded.

"I'm not nice to you," Myra said.

Ms. V. raised an eyebrow in response to her statement.

"I mean what were you… Why did you?" Myra stopped, seeming to flounder.

"Why did I come to you?" Ms. V. asked trying to help the conversation along.

"Yeah."

"You were hurting…are hurting. What type of person would I be if I just let you stand there in pain?" Ms. V. thought she would get a nod of agreement, but instead, Myra's face crumpled. Ms. V. looked around fruitlessly for more tissue but saw some napkins on a nearby table. Before she could get up Madison reached over and picked them up and handed them to her before going back to her own seat. Ms. V. placed the stack of napkins in front of Myra.

"If it were someone else, I would have left them standing there," Myra said, half sobbing. She held the tissue up to her mouth for a moment before continuing. "I would have just watched while I wondered what was so wrong that someone would start crying in the middle of the room." Myra began crying into her tissue, and Ms. V. just waited for the new cycle of sobs to subside. "What…what does that say about me?" Myra asked.

There is no way I'm going to answer that.

"Really. I'm serious. What's wrong with me?" Myra's whispered tone caused Ms. V. to lean in closer.

Ms. V. considered Myra's question more seriously and reached out to listen to what the Holy Spirit was saying.

"Sometimes when people are in a great deal of pain, it's hard for them to notice other people's pain. It can't be labeled a good or bad thing, but it renders the person incapable of helping anyone else."

Ms. V. hoped Myra wouldn't be offended by her response though she tried to keep her words as objective as possible.

"Aren't you ever in pain?" Myra asked.

"Yes, I am. I'm human, but I see an end to my pain. Whether it is emotional pain or physical pain I trust that no matter how bad it is, God my Father will take care of it."

"Why? How do you know?" Myra asked.

"Because God said He would, and He doesn't lie or fail," Ms. V. said.

"But what if He does fail?" Myra asked, not meeting Ms. V.'s eyes

"What do you mean?"

"He didn't keep my father from dying after years of suffering. He didn't heal him," Myra said almost defiantly.

"Oh, child. I am so sorry that you have been separated from your father." Ms. V. said, wanting to reach for the woman again.

Myra broke down and Ms. V. gave in to the urge to hug her again. She spoke soothing words in her ear and prayed,

"Dear Lord, touch the heart of your child. Comfort her and soothe the deepest part of her pain. Give her peace Lord and let her know that she is not alone. In the darkest hours of the night, be with her and comfort her. Dispatch her ministering angels around and about her and speak love into her heart. I ask that for each offense she forgives, that you give her peace, joy, contentment and a new love for herself because she is worth being loved."

Myra gave Ms. V. an embarrassed smile before looking around as if she were trying to see if they were being watched.

Ms. V. saw Madison quickly look the other way as if she weren't keeping track of their every move or leaning in to read lips.

"I was only coming in to get the lunch bag I left in here yesterday. You know Mr. Steinberg. If you leave your food in the refrigerator for more than twenty-four hours, he considers it up for grabs."

Ms. V. nodded in agreement. She had been a victim of Mr. Steinberg's penchant for eating other people's food as well.

"When I walked into the lounge and everyone was having such a wonderful time, I got angry. How could people still be happy when I was so miserable? It wasn't fair. My dad just died, and people were walking around smiling. It felt like you all waited until the worst day of my life to throw a party."

"Honey, you know we didn't know right?"

"Yes. But it didn't make it better."

"I know that if the office had shared about the death of your father, we might have brought food to your home instead of having a potluck here," Ms. V. said

"I don't think so. These people don't know me. They wouldn't care."

"Really? That's not what I just experienced. No one sat there and laughed or talked about you while you cried in the doorway. Instead, everyone got up and embraced you and prayed for you, not knowing what was wrong. Just that you were in pain and needed comforting"

Myra seemed reluctant but she finally nodded. "Do you think they care?"

"I believe it's safe to say that they more than care. You're a part of this school and therefore you're a part of this family."

The school bell rang startling both women and Madison appeared back at Ms. V.'s side. "Myra, I just wanted to tell you, that no matter what it is, I am praying for you and if you need anything, you have my permission to use my number."

"Really?" Myra asked.

Ms. V. stood up. "Like I told you. We are family. I have to go. I have a session right after lunch, but I will be available all of tomorrow morning if you'd like to talk, and you have permission to use my number as well."

"Thank you…for everything."

"That's what family does child. Now go and get your food. I see Mr. Steinberg ambling towards the refrigerator."

She and Madison gave Myra one last hug and walked from the teacher's lounge.

Chapter 10

Death and life are in the power of the tongue: and they that love it shall eat the fruit thereof.
Proverbs 18:21

"...how powerful the words we speak are."

Ms. V. was both energized and exhausted by the day's events thus far, and she still had an important session with brother and sister Joel and Jordan Green. Twins, in fact, who had attended school together all of their lives, including Center of Hope Academy.

Ms. V. had gone over Jordan's file the day before and skimmed over it again now, looking for any causes for concern. At seventeen, Jordan was at the top of her class with her brother. She had a 4.4 G.P.A., and loved science, math and helping people. In their last session, Jordan had voiced her desire to go medical school and become a surgeon beyond the borders of the United States. Ms. V. thought it was both ambitious and selfless, especially since Jordan also planned to go to seminary so she could share God's message and "Heal souls as she healed bodies" as Jordan put it.

Jordan always seemed like a very confident and self-sufficient young woman, but not once had she attended a session without her twin brother, Joel. Joel too had big aspirations, but they leaned towards outer and inner space. Joel wanted to become a psychologist to astronauts, and navy submariners who remained underwater for more than six months at a time. In a former session,

Joel told her that their uncle Eduardo suffered from post-traumatic stress disorder or P.T.S.D., and he'd gradually become a recluse. It had hurt Joel greatly since they'd always been so close. Joel wanted to make sure that the debilitating disorder didn't cause other loved ones to try to remove themselves from their family's lives.

He said he was intrigued by the psychological effects of prolonged stays in naturally stressful environments.

With the twins reaching for such different goals, they were soon going to be separated. Jordan was headed to Luke Divinity School of Medicine on the East Coast, and Joel was headed south to a school for naval intelligence.

Ms. V. wondered what the effects of their separation would be on their psyches, and if their individual confidence would be enough to see them through their time apart.

Hearing a knock at the door, Ms. V. looked up from her files and called out for them to come in. Jordan poked her head in first. "Hi Ms. V. I know we are a little early, but we figured since there were two of us, you might want more time with us."

Ms. V. glanced at her clock. "Well, thank you for the extra ten minutes, but I think we should have more than enough time for both of you in this session." Ms. V. beckoned them to come forward with her hand. "Go ahead and close the door behind you, Joel and you two take a seat."

Once they were both seated in front of her desk, Ms. V. took a good look at them. Both young adults were very good-looking, with their cocoa colored skin, big brown eyes set wide apart, straight noses and square chins. Their Puerto Rican and African-American heritage gave them loose curls that seemed to spiral naturally, thick, dark-brown eyebrows and long lashes. They looked very much alike, especially when Jordan wore her curly hair loose and down around her shoulders. Joel had a way of wearing his equally-curly locks that seem to drive some of the girls in school crazy. His curls were much shorter than his sister's, but his hair covered the tops of his ears and the edge of his collar. He wore most of it messy, with some type of hair product that smoothed it down on the sides. Ms. V. had seen a young lady or two stretch their hands towards his head on occasion, but he'd been able to duck out of their way.

Ms. V. brought her attention back to the twins in front of her, who had been waiting patiently for her to begin.

"Shall we start with prayer?" Ms. V. asked and as they bowed their heads, she began.

"Heavenly Father, we thank you for your grace and mercy that has seen us through to this day. I thank you for these two very bright young adults in front of me who are about to embark on the next stages of their lives. I ask that you continue to guide their thoughts throughout this session. Give them clarity and understanding as they share what's in their hearts. In Jesus' name. Amen."

"Amen." The siblings answered simultaneously.

Ms. V. smiled at both of them. "So, who would like to begin?"

"Jordan raised her hand, and Ms. V. turned to her in time to catch her giving Joel a surreptitious look.

"Joel and I have been closer to one another than anyone else," said Jordan. "This has been a hard year for me, knowing that we won't be together after graduation. I know there are phones, video chat, text and email, but I haven't gone more than a day without seeing or being in reach of Jordan. When things get tough and I get out of my head, I know he'll be there to talk some sense into me." She raised her hands when Joel opened his mouth. She wasn't looking at him, but she interrupted him before he could speak. Ms. V. found the exchange extraordinary.

"I know. I know it's up to me to bring myself back to earth now, but I've been considering maybe changing my direction. I love helping people in any circumstance." She took a deep breath, looking deflated.

Ms. V. looked between Jordan and Joel. From Joel's expression, this was not the first time Jordan had shared this. The deep scowl on his face told her that he'd also tried talking to his sister.

"I want to ask you a question, Jordan," Ms. V. said as she picked up a pencil. "How long have you wanted to be a doctor?"

Jordan blinked at Ms. V. a couple of times before answering. "All of my life. Or, at least since I was seven."

"During our last conversation, you told me how hard you've worked to make the grades that would get you into Luke School of Divinity. I suspect your brother has done the same. The two of you are at the top of your class, and your classmates look up to you. Neither one of you, from what I know, are dealing with a lot of emotional baggage with boyfriends and girlfriends. You would give up all of that out of fear?" Ms. V. kept her eyes on Jordan the whole time she spoke.

Jordan didn't fidget, but she did look down as she thought through Ms. V.'s question. The fact that the young lady had to think about her question made Ms. V. consider that there was something more to Jordan's change of heart.

When the teen looked up Ms. V. narrowed her eyes on Jordan and saw more than fear behind her eyes. "What's going on Jordan? Why are you deviating from your plan after all of this time?

Jordan glanced at Joel again, but this time he shook his head with the slightest movement possible. Catching the byplay between them, Ms. V. grew a little impatient.

"I understand that you two are used to handling things on your own, but it is also obvious that you aren't able to take care of this between yourselves. I would like to help, but I can't do that unless you are honest with me."

Joel blew out a huge breath. "Ms. V. my sister has a huge heart. It is too big sometimes."

Jordan sucked her teeth, drawing a stern look from Ms. V., but Joel went on as if he hadn't heard a thing. "Our grandmother moved in with us this year. She is getting older and just didn't want to be alone. Our parents do very well. We have a big home with extra room, so it was logical for her to come stay with us instead of any of our other tias and tios. My father was proud that he could offer her this after our grandfather died, even though it took her six years to accept it.

"Our abuela is wonderful. She cooks breakfast every morning and sometimes dinner if it's a special occasion. She and Jordan are the closest of my younger brothers and sisters and me. I think more than leaving me, she's afraid of leaving our abuela."

Ms. V. took in this information and the look of sadness on Jordan's face, which confirmed both her thoughts and everything Joel had just said.

"Is this true?" Ms. V. asked Jordan, already knowing the answer.

Jordan nodded. Ms. V. slowly exhaled. A child's love for a parent or family member could just as easily encourage them to move toward their dreams as it could to keep them close.

"Jordan, tell me what's going on." Ms. V. prompted.

Jordan sat up in her chair. "Our grandmother isn't getting any younger. I want to spend as much time with her as I can, but I can't do that if I go to school on the other side of the country. If I go with Joel to San Diego, I can at least be closer to her. It's only a two-hour drive. I can do that on the weekends."

"What does your grandmother say?" Ms. V. asked.

Jordan gave a long-suffering sigh before she spoke. "She wants me to go. But what if something happens? What if she gets sick or has…?"

The clap that came from Joel startled both Ms. V. and Jordan. They looked over at him.

"Don't do that. Don't put your mouth on her like that. You know what mama has taught us; how powerful the words we speak are. She has proven it to us time and time again. When Jonah was sick, she only spoke words of healing over him," Joel looked up at Ms. V. "Jonah is our youngest brother. He caught pneumonia when he was three. Our mom forbade us to speak anything but healing and a long life over him even when the doctors said the chances of his recovery was slow due to his immune system not reacting as it should have been. We didn't speak anything but healing and he made a full recovery. The same with our schools. You got into the one you wanted to get into, and I know how concerned you were with the low hours of volunteering you were able to do this year. Still, we only spoke positive words." Joel rubbed his forehead as though he was weary. It reminded Ms. V. of something her father used to do when he was frustrated but wanted to hold back the harsh words. This young man was more mature than she first thought if he was able to hold onto his emotions with such control. Ms. V. glanced over at Jordan. Her head was down, but her posture looked rigid. Obviously, they'd had this conversation, too.

"All I'm saying is don't let your fears talk you into speaking sickness and death over Abuela," Joel continued. "She's healthy and active. She'll be all right." Joel turned to Jordan and took her hand. 'It's not irrational or wrong to want to stay close. I love Abuela too, and I know it's going to be harder for you because you'll be so far away. If I promise to look in on her more often to make sure she's telling you the truth about any aches or pains or more, will that ease your concerns?"

Ms. V. looked to Jordan whose head had come up. Her eyes were still glistening but there was a small smile tipping up the edge of her lips.

"It's a lot to ask. I know you'll be busy. You would do that?"

"Of course, I would. We've been each other's eyes and ears for years. Why won't you trust me to do so now?"

The look that crossed between the two of them spoke volumes.

"How do you think Abuela would feel if you didn't go because of her? She would be heartbroken." Joel's words made things even more plain.

"I wouldn't tell her," Jordan said, eyes narrowed with suspicion.

"You wouldn't have to," Joel said. "She isn't feeble or dense, and she would be so disappointed with you." Jordan was brought to tears again.

Ms. V. pushed the tissue box to the edge of the table and Jordan took a few.

This was one of the easiest sessions Ms. V. had ever held. It seemed they only needed someone to mediate their conversation so they would listen to one another, and even more importantly, know they were being heard.

Ms. V. sat quietly while Joel comforted Jordan. Once her tears had dried Ms. V. asked Jordan some pointed questions.

"So, Jordan, you've listened to Joel and he's listened to you. Do you understand where he's coming from in his reasoning?"

Jordan nodded then looked up at Ms. V. "Yes. I knew he was against me staying, but now that he's explained why he feels that way I understand his opinion."

"How do you feel now about leaving now?" Ms. V. asked

"If it will disappoint mi abuela more than help her, then I will go." Jordan turned to Joel, pointing her finger at him. "But you better tell me if there is anything she tries to hide from me, otherwise I'm coming back."

"Deal," Joel responded.

They both turned to Ms. V. and looked at her expectantly.

Just uncanny. Ms. V. thought to herself.

"Do either of you have any questions on anything else you'd wish to say?"

They both shook their heads to the negative, then seeming to remember her rule about speaking instead of nodding, they answered, "No," in unison.

"Okay. Well. Good." She clapped her hands to call an end to their session.

"Shall we pray?" The siblings bowed their heads and Ms. V. began.

"Dear Heavenly Father, we thank You for your love and adoration. We thank you that we can come to you with anything; what we consider big and small. You want to hear from us. You want to have a personal relationship with us so that you can assuage our doubts, extinguish our fears, and lead us on the straightest and smoothest paths. We thank you for this opportunity.

"Lord, I lift up Joel and Jordan to you. I ask that you continue to lead and guide them with your Holy Spirit. You have given them one another and a close family filled with love. You have given them intelligence and parents to teach them a strong work ethic. They will go far, and they will go even further with You. You have blessed them with a wise mother and an adoring abuela. I ask that you keep them close to You, and to one another as they leave their families to pursue their next level of education. Give them peace as they take separate roads, and give them the comfort they need during this time of transition. We thank you for these gifts and blessings, in Jesus' name, Amen."

Ms. V. took a deep breath, experiencing a sense of completion that was rare in her line of work.

"We have one more session scheduled for the end of the year, but I would like to propose that yours be held separately."

Joel and Jordan glanced at each other, smiling before turning back to Ms. V. and nodding.

"Good. From now on I will hold sessions with each of you separately. I would also suggest that you two begin attending events separately. There is nothing wrong with you hanging out once you arrive, but I want to encourage you to start spending more time with your friends, so when you two part in August it won't be tremendously traumatic for either of you."

Joel looked more confident than Jordan, but Ms. V. expected that. "I'm not saying to avoid one another or go out of your way not to spend time together. I am just encouraging you to spend a little more time with your friends." Ms. V. looked back and forth between the two teens and noted the relief on Jordan's face. Ms. V. glanced at the clock and stood up to come around her desk. "I believe that is it for today."

Jordan and Joel got to their feet.

"Thank you, Ms. V.," Joel said, sliding his arm through the strap of his backpack.

"You're welcome," Ms. V. responded.

"Thank you, Ms. V.," Jordan said, holding her books to her chest. She had a serene smile on her face.

"You're welcome, dear," Ms. V. replied and watched the two walk from her room.

Ms. V. sat back for a moment and contemplated the two teens. She was sure they would be just fine if they held fast to their beliefs and their mother's words. She wasn't sure if they knew just how far ahead they already were but made a vow to herself to continue to pray for them whenever they came to mind.

Ms. V. glanced over at her aquarium, watching the fish swim back and forth, letting their movement soothe her. She gripped the arms of her seat tightly as a wave of dizziness came over her and the sense of floating wouldn't allow her to regain her equilibrium. She was concerned to feel her stomach lurch as the room dipped and swung. The more it swayed, the tighter she held on to keep from falling forward or to either side. She pressed herself against the back of the chair and closed her eyes, hoping to stop the ride her body was taking. The feeling continued, and Ms. V. wondered if she should try to get to her feet. She quickly rejected that thought, knowing she could do herself a great deal of bodily harm. She partially opened one eye to look around her desk. It was hard to put her thoughts in order, let alone get her eye to focus on one specific item. In one shift she saw her phone and reached out a hand in that direction but came up short. She tried again, forcing herself to concentrate through the rolling motion of the room. She leaned forward slowly, working to keep her focus on the receiver handle as the rest of the room fell back in some type of fuzzy tunnel of movement. She squinted through both eyes, inching toward it until she calculated that she was in reach of the device and set her hand down.

The ringing of the phone as her fingers brushed it brought the room back in stark relief. The floor and ceiling realigned themselves and her brain seemed to take back its rightful space in her head, though she knew that was just a feeling. Her fingers shook as she reached for the phone again, and no wonder, after what she just experienced. Her doctor's appointment was the following week, but should she go into urgent care sooner?

Ms. V. picked up the receiver on the third ring and was surprised to hear the steadiness of her voice.

"Hello?"

"Ms. V. This is Myra in the administrative office. You have a delivery. Would you like me to accept it for you, or have the gentleman come to your office?"

Ms. V.'s mind went blank for a moment, trying to match the pleasantness of the speaker's tone with the woman she'd had too many tense conversations with to count. Right before she opened her mouth though she remembered their conversation in the teacher's lounge. *That had been real.* No matter what type of episode she'd just gone through, she could be assured that she at least had been in the teacher's lounge earlier that day.

"Yes. Please have the delivery man bring it to my room." Ms. V. responded, not quite trusting herself to make the walk from her room to the administrative office. "Uh, Are you sure you are feeling well enough to be working? I know you initially called in sick." Ms. V. allowed the rest of her thoughts to go unsaid.

"I decided that I felt better being here than being at home with my thoughts," Myra said, some of the lightness in her tone melting away. Ms. V. thought of addressing the woman's statement but remembered the reason for the call in the first place.

"I understand. Thank you, Myra." Ms. V.'s mouth felt unfamiliar with placing that particular name with the note of gratitude. She wondered at her own part in their antagonistic relationship.

"You're welcome," Myra replied. "I will send him to you right away." Then she hung up.

Ms. V. stared at the receiver for a moment, working through her feelings of surrealism at the odd collection of events. She slowly got to her feet, waiting for another wave of dizziness to hit, but when it didn't she felt confident that she could make it across the room in time to meet the delivery person at the door. She would accept the package and call the office back and let them know she would be leaving early for the day. She would go home, rest, and call her doctor to see if there had been a cancellation. Her predicament might not be an emergency, but it was definitely growing urgent.

Ms. V. opened her door to the deliveryman and accepted the parcel in exchange for her signature. She smiled at the gentleman, preoccupied with her decision to leave.

"Are you well?" the man asked.

Ms. V. blinked at him in confusion. Did her episode show on her face somehow? "Um. I believe so. Don't I look all right?"

"Yes. Sorry. I'm just asking because this is the fourth time I've delivered something for you. From what I can see, you're well liked, but usually I don't have so many deliveries go to one person unless they are... You know what? It was an insensitive question. I was just curious. I'm sure you are loved because from the look of your room, I'm not the only one delivering gifts to you. Have a good day, Miss," he said quickly before backing out of the room.

Ms. V. turned around to see what he meant and noticed that there were vases of flowers, stuffed animals and plants sprinkled throughout the room. No wonder it had begun to smell like a hot house in her office lately.

It wasn't her birthday... Ms. V. pondered the thought for a moment but was distracted by the weighty package in her hand. She slowly walked back to her desk and brought out the scissors.

Once she'd opened the package, the most delightful fragrance met her nose and she inhaled deeply. The soothing scent of lavender enveloped her, and she pulled out a candle. There were two more candles in the box. One was chamomile and the other tea tree. The scents together were cleansing and relaxing and perfect to add as a soothing aid for her bath when she got home.

"Perfect," she said, to no one in particular, as she placed everything back in the box and made a call to the office.

Chapter 11

We are confident, I say, and willing rather to be absent from the body, and to be present with the Lord.
2 Corinthians 5:8

"He merely transitioned from the body to the spirit."

Ms. V. sifted through her files, pulling out the students she would have sessions with that day. It was a particularly gloomy day. The sky had been just a few shades lighter than dusk when she started out for work only lightening a little as she pulled into the school parking lot.

The sound of the rain against the window was distracting rather than relaxing and Ms. V. wondered about her reaction to something that had always calmed her.

She looked up at the knock on her door and called out permission for the people on the other side to enter.

Myra walked in with a bouquet of spring wildflowers. They seemed to bring sunlight with them into the room. Ms. V.'s countenance lightened at the sight, her eyes following the flowers more than Myra for the first few seconds.

"To what do I owe the pleasure of your visit?" Ms. V. asked thinking Myra was delivering the flowers instead of just calling her to come and get them.

As if she'd heard Ms. V.'s thoughts, Myra responded as she set the vase of flowers on Ms. V.'s desk.

"They're from me." Myra gave her a sheepish smile before taking a step back. "I would have given them to you earlier, but you didn't come by the office to get your messages this morning and I was just able to get away."

She hadn't gone by the office. She wondered what her mind had been preoccupied with to throw her off her daily routine, and remembered that she'd been on the phone with one of the members of her church's Sick and Shut-in Committee. They were in the midst of prayer as she entered the school building, and she hadn't wanted to interrupt the prayer to go into the office.

"Phone call," was all Ms. V. said in explanation, and was surprised to see Myra's face brighten. Had Myra thought Ms. V. was avoiding her?

"I've been thinking about what you said yesterday while we were in the teacher's lounge," Myra said. Ms. V. gestured for her to take a seat, which she did readily.

"I was wondering why you responded the way you did when I told you about my father." Myra continued. "Most people just say, "I'm sorry for your loss. Your response stayed in my mind all evening and I was just wondering…" Myra's voice faded as if she were unsure if she should be asking in the first place.

Ms. V. smiled to reassure her. "I have a couple of questions for you of my own before I answer your question. Is that all right?"

Myra nodded her consent.

"Do you think your father is still suffering?"

Myra blinked at her. "Um, no. He's not doing anything anymore."

"But he isn't suffering," Ms. V. said. "He is free from that." She looked at Myra for a moment before asking her next question, not sure if it was too personal. "Do you know if your father believed in God? Do you know if he had given his life to Christ?"

"Yeah. If you lived in his house, you went to church on Sunday." Myra replied without hesitation.

Ms. V. nodded and gave Myra a small smile. "If your father gave his life to Christ and believed Him to be his Lord and Savior then your father is not dead. He merely transitioned from the body to the spirit. He has everlasting life with God. If you also believe in God and have accepted Jesus Christ as your Lord and Savior, you *will* see your father again. You will be with him again. That is why I said it as I did. You didn't lose your father. You are just separated from him. It doesn't make it any less painful, but one big difference is that there is hope." Ms. V. noticed Myra's tears and pushed the ever-ready box of tissues closer to her.

Myra smiled and took one. She dabbed at her eyes and cleared her throat. She looked as though she was deep in thought before she spoke. "I was wondering if you would consider… if you could maybe show me how to…how you…what to do."

"You mean believe in God?" Ms. V. asked.

"Yes, if it'll make me more like you," Myra said.

Ms. V. was at a momentary loss for words. That was the last thing she would have thought she'd hear when she came into the school building that morning. *You are a miracle-working God!*

"Ah, Myra, I don't want you to aim to be like me. That isn't a lofty enough goal for someone as strong as you. I want you to aim to be the very best you that you can be. That is a goal that will take a lifetime to achieve, as it's supposed to. God wouldn't want you to emulate anyone but Him, otherwise you would fall short as I sometimes do."

Myra's face fell and her eyes darted around the room, seeming lost.

Ms. V. leaned forward. "All I'm saying is, please don't use me as a point of destination, but a steppingstone in your relationship with God. I can help you, yes. I can usher you, yes but the rest is up to you. Do you understand?" Ms. V. asked hoping she hadn't gone too far.

"I think so. You said you would help me, right?"

"Yes." Ms. V. nodded and saw Myra's demeanor lighten.

"Good," Myra said.

"Um, do you have a church home now?" Ms. V. asked, thinking that she could commit to sharing scripture with the young woman and talking with her from time to time, but hoping someone from her or her father's church could take her by the hand.

"No. Not really. What church do you go to?" Myra asked, and Ms. V. wondered if the miracle God just worked wasn't a joke on her.

Ms. V. opened her mouth to answer when there was a knock on the door. The sense of relief made her feel bad but as happy as she was at Myra's one-eighty-degree turn, she wasn't sure if she had the energy and wherewithal to lead her by the hand. Ms. V. would be there to encourage her and answer any questions, but she would be praying for God to send someone who could befriend and counsel Myra.

No matter how sweet Myra was at the moment, Ms. V. understood that years of bitterness were the fruit that grew from a tree rooted deep in pain and it would take some time and a great deal of love and patience to uproot it.

"I'm sorry, Myra. Could we continue this conversation a little later?" Ms. V. asked, rising from her desk. She noted the disappointment in Myra's eyes before the young woman got up from her seat.

"Sure. Sure. I just wanted to give you that," Myra said, gesturing to the flowers. "And of course, the question." Myra moved away from the desk without turning around.

"Um, do you think we could sit with each other at lunch? I feel a little self-conscious about going into the teacher's lounge after yesterday," Myra admitted, as they made their way to the door.

Ms. V. could understand her discomfort, but today, of all days, she suspected the teachers would rally around Myra rather than ostracize her. It was Myra's former attitude that would have kept the other teachers at a distance.

"Yes, but I believe you will find that the other teachers will have more to say to you than about you," Ms. V. said just before she opened the door.

"Thank you," Myra said, before giving her and Mr. Sanderson, who was standing on the other side of the threshold, a shy smile. She walked through the door and a puzzled-looking Mr. Sanderson greeted both women.

Ms. V. waited expectantly for Mr. Sanderson to walk in but found herself amused when he continued to stare after Myra.

"Mr. Sanderson." She called to get his attention.

His head snapped back in her direction, a flush darkening his neck.

"Did you need something?" Ms. V. asked as she watched Mr. Sanderson look back one more time before seeming to realize that he was at her door. The confused expression was still on his face.

"Um, yes, sorry. I came by to give you a praise report. I didn't mean to interrupt you," Mr. Sanderson said, looking a little off-balance before he visibly shook his head and directed his focus on Ms. V. He rubbed his forehead for a second as if it would help organize his thoughts.

"You didn't interrupt. Would you like to come in? I can always use some good news," Ms. V. stepped back then lead him over to the lounge area of her room.

"I haven't seen you for a few weeks," Ms. V. asked, as they sat down on the couches. "I take it, you went to see your sister after all?" Ms. V."

Mr. Sanderson smiled sadly. "I did. I prayed first though. That took about a week in itself. I was torn between wanting to see her to make sure she was okay and what God wanted me to do."

"How is Margaret…and Peter? Is it?" Ms. V. asked, wanting to make sure she had Mr. Sanderson's sister and brother-in-law's names correct.

"They are both doing well actually, and yes you're correct." Mr. Sanderson rubbed his hands together as he sat across from Ms. V. A small smile played across his lips. "In fact, you were correct in a few ways, but I'm getting ahead of myself," Mr. Sanderson said, leaning back on the sofa. "After I left your office I went home and called one of the ministers at my church. I remembered that he worked in the healthcare field. What part, I couldn't remember, but when we spoke, he informed me that he was a rheumatologist. He gave me a different perspective and some insight into what my sister and brother-in-law might be going through.

"He sent me some literature on the effects of chemotherapy, and I sat back and did some research while I prayed for direction in that first week. It calmed me and gave me the reassurance I needed. I found that by gaining the knowledge I did, I was less susceptible to giving in to the fear I'd been struggling with." Mr. Sanderson gave Ms. V. a sheepish look as if to say that she had been right in praying against fear, but it was more for *his* benefit than his sibling and her husband.

"When I finally went to visit Margaret, she looked much better than I suspected she would. She was surprised, of course because I hadn't warned her that I was coming. She seemed genuinely pleased to see me, though.

"Anyway, for the first few days I just observed and kind of followed her around as she went through her routine. I didn't try to step in and change things. I just helped when she said she needed a hand. It was a good visit. She did confess, though, that she was happy I chose to come that week and not the one before. She was more recovered from her last session of chemotherapy and able to get around better, whereas the previous week she said she'd needed to remain in bed a couple of days." Mr. Sanderson released a long exhale. "Her admission went a long way into assuaging my concerns. It looks like she has things under control, as she said." Mr. Sanderson gave her a small shrug and a grin.

"As Margaret said she did from the beginning," Ms. V. reiterated with a smile she didn't try to hide.

"As she said she did from the beginning," Mr. Sanderson agreed, grinning back.

"So, what does that mean for your career?" Ms. V. asked, sensing Mr. Sanderson's relief, but reconsidered the thought as his brows furrowed at her question.

"I guess I'm back where I was when we first talked. Funny thing though, at the time, it seemed like such an important option when I weighed it against going to take care of my sister and brother-in-law. Now that the outlook on my sister's life isn't as precarious as I first assumed, I can go back to concentrating on my career... only." Mr. Sanderson paused and stared off into space for a few seconds before seeking out her gaze again. "I find that it doesn't seem as important. I would like to be principal, but during my visit with my sister, I realized that I was missing something. Now that I'm back here, alone, it seems clear. "

"What seems clear?" Ms. V. asked.

"It seems clear that my career isn't enough. I want more...maybe a family of my own."

Ms. V. was surprised by the turn of the conversation but absorbed Mr. Sanderson's words and her mind turned to his distraction at seeing Myra.

"Do you have anyone in mind?" Ms. V. asked, hoping she was wrong.

"No. It's a pretty recent revelation," Mr. Sanderson said. "I just thought I would share it because as a single woman I figured you would understand."

"Understand what?" Ms. V. didn't want to seem coy, but she enjoyed living alone. She was so rarely at home, if she thought about it. There was her work at the school, as well as her ministry work and occasional after-hour family counseling and mentoring.

"The loneliness. The need to connect to just one person above all else?" Mr. Sanderson looked at her intently.

Ms. V. began to feel uncomfortable, not because she thought Mr. Sanderson had any type of interest in her, but because he was touching on some very personal aspects of her life that she wasn't sure she wanted to discuss. She watched him for a few heartbeats before speaking.

"I'm content with my life, but I understand that desire. I had the same wish once…" Ms. V. stopped herself from speaking and shut off the memories that tried to tag along. "What does this mean for you?" Ms. V. continued quickly, so Mr. Sanderson didn't have a chance to ask her about her comment.

Mr. Sanderson watched her for a second or two before answering her question. "I don't know, really. I guess I am just opening myself up to options I didn't consider before," His words sounded somewhat reluctant.

Ms. V. didn't want him to think that her desires for herself were something she was putting on him. "I think that's a very good idea. I believe your visit with Margaret and Peter, on the whole, has given you new insight and a different perspective. You might have been too preoccupied with your work to consider these things before. Life has so much to offer when it comes to family, friends and romantic relationships. I think you would be cheating yourself if you denied the opportunity to explore some of the greatest gifts God has given us." The wariness left Mr. Sanderson's expression and Ms. V. saw his eyes soften in agreement and his shoulders relax.

"Thank you, Ms. V.," he said, looking around her room. "I can't tell you how much your advice has meant to me. I can understand why you have so many flowers and gifts in your office. You are such an integral part of this school. I'm glad that people are showing you how much they appreciate you." Mr. Sanderson finished with a bright smile. He took a deep breath before getting up from the couch.

"I'm not going to take up any more of your precious time. I know you have to get ready for a session with one of your students.

I just wanted to share that with you; thank you again for lending me your spiritual ear and giving me those words of wisdom."

"You're welcome, Mr. Sanderson. Please feel free to keep me updated regarding your sister and brother-in-law, and your new outlook on life."

"I will. I promise," he answered as they walked to the door.

Ms. V. had two seconds to hope that she might get a few minutes to herself between the time Mr. Sanderson placed his hand on the doorknob and opened it to find Samantha on the other side.

Well, so much for that hope.

"Blessings upon you, Mr. Sanderson," Ms. V. said.

"Indeed, they are, Ms. V." Mr. Sanderson returned.

Chapter 12

For am I now seeking the approval of man, or of God? Or am I trying to please man? If I were still trying to please man, I would not be a servant of Christ.
Galatians 1:10

"...to lead by example for people who are quick to judge..."

Ms. V. gave Mr. Sanderson a farewell smile as he stepped aside to allow Samantha to enter. She felt light after her discussion with Mr. Sanderson and hoped to use some of that positive energy during her session with Samantha. She hadn't completely recovered from her bout of weakness from the day before, even with the long soak and aromatherapy candles, but Mr. Sanderson's praise report went a long way in lifting her spirit.

"Good morning, Samantha, it's good to see you," Ms. V. said, watching the young lady for any expression that would tell her how the teen was doing. It had been two weeks since the parent/student session she'd moderated for Samantha and her parents, Pastor and Mrs. Royce.

Ms. V. had realized right away that she would have to be very careful to show her objectivity in the session. Pastor Royce was even more charismatic and charming than he was after his weekly services, which was saying a great deal. Ms. V. could tell that the more her father turned up the charisma, the more solemn Samantha became, until it had become almost impossible to coax multi-syllable words out of her. Samantha's mother remained quiet, though her expression became more concerned as Samantha's attitude soured.

They were fifteen minutes into the session when Ms. V. asked Pastor Royce point-blank if he understood the reason for the session Ms. V. had called. As she could have predicted, Pastor Royce placed the blame for the session on his daughter's unsatisfactory performance in her classes. Ms. V. quickly dispelled him of that notion.

"Pastor Royce, we're here this evening because after meeting with Samantha two weeks ago, she and I thought it might be easier for her to express her emotions and feel as though she was being heard if we all met together." Ms. V. could tell right away that her statement wasn't as well received as she hoped. Pastor Royce's lips thinned, and he pointedly looked over at Samantha who seemed to cower under his gaze.

Ms. V. had seen this silent type of manipulation before. It stifled conversation, even as the person taking charge of the discussion looked outwardly open to accepting the other person's views.

In certain cases, Ms. V. had given her students the opportunity to take the initiative and express themselves in a respectful and honest manner. It worked when the parents were honestly open to hearing what their child had to say. In this instance, she knew the pastor's looks were meant to intimidate Samantha so that she either remained silent or blew up. Neither of those responses would give the teen the outcome Ms. V. knew she was seeking.

"Well, I don't have a Ph.D. in psychology or counseling, so forgive me for my ignorance, but wouldn't Samantha need to give more than monosyllabic answers for that to happen?" Pastor Royce asked as he looked back and forth between Ms. V. and Samantha.

The heat rising in Ms. V. chest was more than enough warning for her to take charge of the conversation.

"Pastor Royce, Samantha's quietness at this moment in no way represents her feelings, otherwise there would be no need for us to be having this discussion. Your daughter is hurting and in distress to the degree that she was willing to fail out of school just to get your attention." Ms. V. took a deep breath.

Mrs. Royce's expression of concern grew to alarm then anxiousness. The vestiges of Pastor Royce's charm, genuine or otherwise, faded and a hardness came over his features for a second that surprised Ms. V. It didn't remain more than a second or two, but it gave Ms. V. even more of a glimpse into the man behind the robe outside of the church on Sundays. She was not impressed and had to work even harder to stay objective.

"Is this true Samantha?" Pastor Royce asked. Before Samantha could open her mouth, he continued. "Were you intentionally trying to fail out of school and waste not only our money but the money of the members of our church who see fit to donate to your education?"

"Pastor Royce." Ms. V. interjected. "I don't think this is the time to…"

Pastor Royce held up his hand to silence Ms. V. and she had to work not to pull rank at that moment because she couldn't trust her words not to convey her disappointment in the man.

"I think she needs to know what she is playing with when she pulls stunts like this," Pastor Royce said. "She can't put her future at risk when she doesn't get her way."

Ms. V. didn't even look at Samantha; instead, she took the opportunity Pastor Royce had just offered to get back on the subject.

"Pastor Royce, what do you believe is the cause for what you may consider Samantha's rebellious behavior?" Ms. V. asked, leading Pastor Royce and thus the conversation. Ms. V. saw Samantha shift in her seat and hoped the teen wouldn't give up and leave before she could reset the environment.

Pastor Royce leaned back in his chair, his demeanor one of a person who was confident in their opinion. "Samantha is a very intelligent girl. Sometimes I think she is too intelligent for her own good. She doesn't have to work hard to maintain an A or B average and subjects come easy for her. I think it causes her to become lax and lazy. It comes off in her demeanor and her appearance." Pastor Royce looked over at his daughter before returning Ms. V.'s gaze.

"We've talked about her attire," he continued. "I've even encouraged her to go shopping with her mother to choose clothing that would better represent this family as the head of our church." Pastor Royce finished with a heavy sigh.

Ms. V. turned to Mrs. Royce. "Is there anything you would like to add?"

Mrs. Royce's glance flickered between Pastor Royce and Samantha before she looked back at Ms. V. "I'm disappointed that Samantha chose to place her academic future in jeopardy instead of sitting down and having a mature conversation with us, but I hope we can resolve some of the issues this evening."

Ms. V. was also disappointed that Samantha hadn't felt that she could confide in her mother and needed to resort to such drastic measures.

She turned to Samantha, making sure her expression held nothing but support and encouragement. "Samantha, this is your opportunity to share with your parents what we discussed two weeks ago."

Samantha sat up straight in her chair and licked her lips as though her mouth had gone dry. She glanced down at the hem of her oversized sweater and inhaled sharply.

Ms. V. saw Pastor Royce shift in his chair, crossing one leg over the other. She turned her head without taking her eyes from Samantha for a couple of seconds. She then glanced down at his legs and back to Samantha in a dismissive gesture used to disarm any intimidation brought on by his movement.

Samantha swallowed. "Do you remember the agreement we made last year regarding my classes and piano lessons?" She asked her father, looking him in the eye.

Pastor Royce looked confused.

"The agreement we made where you said if I kept my grades up and learned to play well enough for the choir, I would be able to play on Sundays for praise and worship." Samantha elaborated.

"Yes, but you can't expect me to keep my end of our agreement when you haven't kept up yours." Pastor Royce said, unruffled.

"But you didn't," Samantha responded quickly then inhaled slowly before continuing. "You didn't keep your side of the agreement." Samantha slowly reiterated her statement as if coaxing an injured lion to give her its paw. Ms. V. watched Pastor Royce closely out of the corner of her eye to make sure he didn't try to interrupt or quietly silence the teen. She was pleased when he remained quiet and still.

"I came to you at the end of last semester, after the school concert where I played the piano. Do you remember?" Samantha asked and waited.

Pastor Royce's expression grew taut and Ms. V. saw his jaw flex before he answered. "Yes."

"And you told me that, because of the way I dressed, I wouldn't be able to play on Sunday mornings."

"Yes," Pastor Royce said, through gritted teeth.

"I did everything we agreed upon, but because you didn't approve of my clothing, you went back on your word," Samantha said, in a surprisingly calm tone.

"I am your father, not your business partner or one of your schoolmates. It's my job to keep you from harm, even if that means shielding you from talk and judgment from others. We are the head family of our church and must lead by example." Pastor Royce responded with what looked like genuine emotion. Ms. V. was just relieved that he wasn't hiding behind his persona any longer.

"So, you're saying you won't keep your promise to me because our family has to lead by example for people who are quick to judge and easily hindered by what they see?" Samantha asked quietly, her attitude replaced with bafflement.

Ms. V. turned to Pastor Royce, unable to hide her curiosity at his answer to Samantha's question, noticing Mrs. Royce doing the same. A myriad of expressions crossed Pastor Royce's features, including calculation, consideration and finally resignation.

"No. That's not what I'm trying to communicate to you. I don't want you putting people's judgment above your passion to serve God." Pastor Royce rubbed his hand along his forehead, looking suddenly very tired.

"I think you play exceptionally well, but I've seen some changes in you beyond the difference in appearance and before I can, in good conscience, agree to have you play on Sunday mornings, I need you to answer my next question honestly." Pastor Royce delivered the statement with such solemnity, Ms. V. had an inkling of what he'd been fearing from the beginning.

Good. They were finally getting to the root of the matter.

"I've never known you to be openly defiant," he said. "And you know that our church members show a portion of their reverence to God in their attire on Sunday, so it causes me to believe that your drastic change in appearance is more than just a preference, but a statement of some kind. What is really behind your change in dress?"

Samantha licked her lips again. She averted her eyes for a moment and Ms. V. was afraid she wouldn't open up, but when she looked back up at her father, there was a spark of something in her eyes Ms. V. couldn't read, and tension washed over her.

"Minister Benson," Samantha said before going quiet again. Ms. V. grew still, not allowing herself to jump to conclusions. She glanced at Pastor Royce, who wore a puzzled expression on his face.

"What about Minister Benson?" Mrs. Royce asked, drawing all their attention to her.

Ms. V. was surprised to see how tense the woman had become; her face was tight and her eyes were narrowed. Did she know something?

Samantha stared at her mom then burst into tears. Ms. V. reached over and handed Samantha the box of tissue. The silence in the room was heavy as Samantha dried her tears and worked to regain her composure.

Ms. V. turned to Pastor Royce. "This Minister Benson. Is he a leader in your church?"

Pastor Royce turned to her, confusion still clear on his face. "Yes. *She* is one of our youth ministers."

Ms. V. thought she heard him wrong. "Minister Benson is a woman?"

"Yes. Minister Shirley Benson," Pastor Royce said, sounding preoccupied. "She joined our church two years ago from a church in Blair, Nebraska. Her papers were in order and I was told by her pastor that she was in good standing."

"What about Minister Benson, Samantha?" Mrs. Royce asked.

Samantha hesitated before beginning. "I thought she was just really friendly, being from the Midwest and all. I thought when she invited me to have dinner with her and a few other girls that she was just wanting to get to know us better. She seemed fun and relatable for someone her age. She seemed to get us." Samantha's pleading look at her father broke Ms. V.'s heart.

Samantha went on. "She would hold monthly sleepovers and I attended for a while." She grew quiet for a moment, turning pale. "I even encouraged other girls to come."

"Did something happen during the sleepovers?" Mrs. Royce asked, an edge to her voice Ms. V. wouldn't have guessed the woman possessed earlier.

"It was fine at first. We would have discussions about anything and everything. She was open and answered all our questions. Even the ones most of our elders wouldn't answer." Samantha said looking at her hands as she squeezed them and wrapped them around one another.

Ms. V. had to give it to Samantha's parents. They waited for Samantha, not urging or pushing her to answer before she was ready.

"After a few months though, it became...uncomfortable. She started asking us, me in particular, about boys, and if there was anyone I was interested in. When I told her there was no one special; that I was concentrating on school and my music lessons, she said she didn't believe me. She said I was too beautiful and intelligent not to have a boyfriend." Samantha swallowed, and Ms. V. could hear it from where she was sitting. The knots forming in her stomach threatened to make an appearance with her lunch.

"She also hinted that girls without boyfriends at my age, usually had girlfriends," Samantha said. The eerie silence returned to the room and Ms. V. gripped the sides of her chair to keep silent.

"I thought," Samantha paused to take a breath. "I thought she was just being nosy, but she started saying things before and after services that made me feel uncomfortable. She looked at me in an odd way. I can't explain it, but I stopped going to the sleepovers. It seemed to make her angry, so I started avoiding her whenever I could.

She would make remarks about how I was teasing men and boys alike with my skirts and fitted tops. Then one Sunday she cornered me in the women's bathroom."

Ms. V. saw Pastor Royce grip the arms of his chair, his knuckles bleached of color.

"She stepped really close, backing me up against the wall. I didn't know why she would do such a thing until...until she touched my chest and whispered that she could see my bra through my blouse. I didn't know if she was punishing me, or something else."

"Why didn't you come to us? Why didn't you say anything before now?" Pastor Royce asked, seeming unable to come to terms with everything she was saying.

"Because I didn't think you would believe me," Samantha said.

"Why? What made you think we wouldn't believe you?"

"Because that was the Sunday you presented her with the Minister of the Year Award." Samantha shrugged. "I thought it would be my word against hers since she was such a major part of the ministry." Ms. V. heard the trace of accusation in her voice.

"But you're our daughter," Mrs. Royce said, her voice full of concern as she reached for Samantha's hand. Samantha shrugged but allowed her mother to keep hold of her hand.

"Were there more encounters with this woman?" Pastor Royce asked, his voice sharp and raw with emotion. Ms. V. saw his Adam's apple bob with his swallow.

Samantha shook her head before answering, and Ms. V. felt an overpowering urge to slump in her chair in relief. "She still gives me looks, but I make sure I never go anywhere around the church alone. And that's why I started dressing in layers." Samantha folded her hands in her lap.

Ms. V. inhaled deeply to get her bearings before looking at Pastor Royce and then Mrs. Royce. Both parents looked a little stunned, but Ms. V. was happy they didn't doubt what their daughter told them.

"This woman has been terrorizing our daughter, Eustice." Mrs. Royce said, disgust and loathing warring for domination on her features.

Pastor Royce continued to stare at his daughter as if Mrs. Royce hadn't spoken. The pain and anger in his gaze made Ms. V. shiver. She would have shrunk back when he got up out of his chair if she hadn't seen the sheen of moisture in his eyes. He stepped forward, pulling his daughter out of her seat and into a hug that even from where Ms. V. was sitting, looked painfully tight.

"I'm sorry, Pumpkin. I'm so sorry I didn't protect you." Pastor Royce said, his eyes closed, and cheek pressed to Samantha's temple. Samantha wrapped her arms around her father just as fiercely as her body shook with sobs.

Ms. V. offered the tissue box to Mrs. Royce without looking away from the two hugging in front of her then took a couple from the box for herself when her vision grew blurry with tears.

When they parted, Mrs. Royce got up to embrace her daughter as well. Pastor Royce assured Samantha that he would make things right and when Samantha sat back down in her chair, he didn't move from her side. Ms. V. took it as a good sign that he was acting so protective and possessive. She hoped it would reassure Samantha and begin healing the rift between them.

Feeling that the most intense part of the conversation was over, Ms. V. took the opportunity to ask Samantha what she was sure was on both Pastor and Mrs. Royce's minds as well. "I can understand you dressing in layers as a form of defense on Sundays, but why during the week? Almost since the beginning of the school year, you have dressed in layers or in masculine clothing. May I ask why?"

Samantha glanced at Ms. V. and winced before exhaling slowly. "I was asked out by one of the boys in my history class at the beginning of my sophomore year. He's a bit of a jerk, so I told him no. He didn't like it, and started doing little things like pushing my books off my desk when he walked by and making embarrassing noises behind me. You know, really mature stuff." Samantha added, rolling her eyes. "I knew if I told the teacher things would only get worse, and he never touched me, so I ignored him until he started talking about me to some of his friends. My friend Brenda told me she'd overheard him telling some guy that I was too easy to be worth his time. Which is a lie." Samantha stopped speaking for a moment and Ms. V. got the feeling that she was trying to regain control of her anger before continuing. Her heart went out to this young lady who had gone through so much. Ms. V. took note of the class and semester and was going to see if the teacher remembered any trouble the boy may have caused.

Samantha rubbed her hands up and down her arms before she cleared her throat and sat up straighter. "I confronted him during lunch a couple of weeks later and told him, in front of his friends, the reason why I wouldn't go out with him was that he wasn't my type since he was a liar and a jerk. I hoped it was enough to embarrass him a little and keep him from talking about me, but it kind of backfired and word got around that the type I really didn't like was boys. Instead of fighting it I just started dressing the way one would expect someone who liked girls to dress. It kept most of the boys away and with what was happening with Minister Benson I just felt more comfortable dressing this way." Samantha glanced at Ms. V. before glancing at her parents. Ms. V. caught their looks of anger and dismay as they turned to her.

Ms. V. understood their response and tried to think of a way to handle the situation so it didn't make things worse for Samantha.

"Who is this boy?" Pastor Royce asked, puffed up and sounding indignant.

"Just that," said Ms. V. "A boy who didn't know how to deal with rejection. If I may, I'd like your permission to deal with this. I will make sure it's resolved so that nothing comes back on Samantha."

Samantha began to look uncomfortable. "Do I have to give you his name?"

"That would help, but if you don't wish to, I can always ask your history teacher," Ms. V. said quietly and watched Samantha blanch.

"I don't want to get anyone else involved. The less people who know, the better." The young woman sighed. "It was Kevin Marsh, but he hasn't bothered me at all this semester. Not since he got a girlfriend. But his friends still give me looks and whisper something every now and then."

Ms. V. recognized the name, and her heart turned over in her chest. Kevin Marsh was Porcha Grant's boyfriend. *Sometimes this school could be very small.* Ms. V. would have to be very careful how she navigated through this. She could easily make the assumption that Kevin's absence would solve the issues in two of her student's lives, but the absence of pressure or trials didn't necessarily bring automatic peace. Ms. V. would be calling Kevin Marsh in for an overdue session.

Ms. V. assured Pastor and Mrs. Royce, as well as Samantha, that she would speak with Kevin, but wouldn't mention Samantha specifically. She told them he was due for a session with her soon anyway and she would try to get to the bottom of the matter. Once she received a nod from all three in the room, Ms. V. made herself a note to schedule a meeting with Kevin.

Ms. V. asked Samantha if there was anything else she wanted to discuss, and with the negative shake of the young lady's, head Ms. V. considered the session a victory. The agreement between Samantha and her father regarding whether or not she would play for any services might have to be shifted to the background until the crux of the matter was dealt with. Ms. V. asked them if they wanted to schedule another session with her, and the family agreed that it would be needed but that Samantha could meet with Ms. V. alone first.

Ms. V. prayed for Samantha, Mrs. Royce and Pastor Royce individually and collectively before dismissing the session. She went home that evening feeling a deep sense of accomplishment. The fact that the Lord not only had a hand on the family, but that they were willing to let His perfect will be done, made for a very promising outcome.

Chapter 13

Let your light so shine before men, that they may see your good works, and glorify your Father which is in heaven.
Matthew 5:16

"I didn't start out trying to evangelize."

Now as Samantha sat across from Ms. V., she could see the transformation that had begun on the inside of the young lady on that day two weeks ago. Samantha's eyes were clear and full of the hope Ms. V. had seen in them during her freshman school year. Samantha's clothing, though no longer baggy, was still on the more masculine side, but Ms. V. knew some scars resulting from body-shaming took longer to heal than others. There were no accessories or stylized curls in Samantha's hair, but she'd opted for a natural look that wasn't as severe. It fit her features nicely and made it look as though Samantha was coming out of hiding.

"How are you, Samantha?" Ms. V. asked as she situated herself at her desk.

"Good, Ms. V. I'm doing good. Ms. Rice and Mr. Mapleton let me turn my homework in late. Thank you for speaking to them." Samantha went on and Ms. V. was happy to let her continue. The young lady's animated speech was a balm to Ms. V.'s soul. "I won't get full credit for them because that wouldn't be fair to the other students, but since I can show proof of doing all of the work, I will only be docked one grade. I can still finish the semester with a B average."

"Good for you. I'm very happy that you and your teachers were able to come up with a solution that worked for all of you. How is your family doing?" Ms. V. asked.

Samantha's expression grew thoughtful. "It was pretty intense for a while there, but it's much better now. Dad dismissed Minister Benson." Samantha paused as she raised her eyebrows, giving Ms. V. a pointed look. "He didn't call her out in public, but I'm sure the rumor mill is working overtime since no one knew she was leaving." Samantha continued, before placing her thumbnail in her mouth then snatching it out quickly as if she'd been caught doing something she wasn't supposed to be doing. "He's scheduling sessions with all of the youth and their parents to see if she hurt them in any way. I wouldn't want to be the one that had to do that, but Mom says it's important to offer them the same opportunity to heal as you gave us." Samantha finished with a smile.

"All I did was try and give you a safe environment to share your feelings," said Ms. V. "It's my job. I'm just thankful that we caught this when we did. You are a very brave young lady. It couldn't have been easy for you to share with your parents what had been going on with Minister Benson. If you didn't open up and speak to them during this session, it could have gone on for much longer and we don't know how many children could have been impacted." As Ms. V. said the words, she felt truly thankful to God for giving Samantha the strength to break the silence.

Ms. V. noted the flush on Samantha's cheeks and just waited for the teen to get past her embarrassment.

Samantha scooted to the edge of her seat, a brightness entering her eyes. "So, I start rehearsing with the choir tomorrow evening. I'm so excited. I won't be able to play during Sunday service until after my report card shows my improvement, but that isn't too far away." Samantha smiled, letting the sentence fade.

Ms. V. studied the young lady and reassessed her first judgment of Samantha's attire. Her clothing may still cover her from chin to ankle, but the glow coming from her eyes couldn't be hidden under any clothing or makeup. Ms. V. was glad to see her so happy.

They spoke for another half-hour about Samantha's plans for the summer and upcoming year, and about the group of teens she'd been associating with. It turned out that Samantha wanted to invite them to her church, but not while Minister Benson was there. She had been slowly evangelizing and answering questions they had regarding the Old Testament laws and the fulfillment of those laws in the New Testament.

"I didn't start out trying to evangelize," Samantha said as if she were afraid Ms. V. would take her previous statement wrong. "I actually wanted someplace to be alone so I could find some peace. It turns out that the place I found was also where they got together to work on a graphic novel they've been creating for teens and young adults. But you didn't hear that from me." Samantha said the last part conspiratorially as she leaned in closer.

Ms. V. couldn't deny her surprise but worked to hide both her smile and her wonder. It looked like she'd been doing some judging of her own.

"So, is this a Christian-based graphic novel?" Ms. V. asked, curious.

"I'm sorry. I can't tell you more than I already have. I promised." Samantha sounded apologetic but resolved.

Ms. V. conceded and didn't try to get any more information out of the teen. She nodded at Samantha before moving to the next subject. "How's it going with the other members of the student body?" Ms. V. asked referring to Kevin Marsh and his friends.

Ms. V. had taken the opportunity to discuss a few subjects with him under the guise of his senior exit session, including any 'rumors' she'd heard regarding his behavior with some of the female students that school year. It had been interesting, to say the least.

Kevin Marsh was an insecure teen with home issues that had spilled out into every part of his life. Their exit session had become a two-parter, and Ms. V. had learned that Kevin's behavior was partly in response to some of the frustration and pain he had regarding his parent's separation and subsequent divorce.

She was relieved to learn that Kevin's feelings for Porcha were true, but his experiences with his parent's marriage were causing him to feel vulnerable and to have second thoughts about his relationship with her. It didn't solve all of Kevin's problems, but by the time their second session was over Kevin had talked out most of his disappointments and insecurities. He'd even brought up his feelings of regret for some of his antics earlier in the school year, which allowed Ms. V. another opening to gaining some restitution for Samantha.

"I think it will get better soon," Samantha replied, referring to Kevin. "If I'm not imagining it, I think the weird looks from some of Kevin's friends have stopped. Brenda said she heard from Sandra Price in third period that Kevin told one of his friends before class that he was wrong, and I was pretty decent." Samantha smiled.

"Pretty decent." Ms. V. said. "That's good?"

"Yeah," Samantha said as if Ms. V. should have known. "If he said I was more than that, I might have gotten some backlash from his girlfriend or her friends."

"So, you're good with that?" Ms. V. asked, to confirm that Samantha was happy with the results.

"Yes. My reputation has been restored to what it was before." Samantha shrugged. "Whatever that was."

Ms. V. stared at her for a moment to make sure Samantha was telling the truth about her satisfaction with the situation. With one more blink Ms. V. let the subject go.

"Okay." she nodded before going on. "How's your relationship with your father?" Ms. V. knew she would be remiss in her job if she didn't ask.

Samantha began with a shrug. "It's okay. It's better." She let out a long exhale. "He's very protective. He won't let me out of his sight when we are around the church and he picks me up from school every day now. Before, he would at least let me take the bus. I get it, and in some ways I feel safer, but I hope this doesn't last through my senior year, otherwise I'll have to choose a college far away." Samantha chuckled.

Ms. V. shared a smile with her. "Be easy on him. It's hard to think that someone could get to those you love. He's going to be dealing with some of that guilt for a while, but he has one great thing going for him."

Samantha tipped her head to the side. "What's that?"

"He has God. If he uses this as a chance to draw closer to God and receive the healing he needs, he will come out of this a better man, a better father and a better pastor."

Samantha seemed to consider her words before she finally nodded in agreement.

With nothing more to discuss before the whole family met with her again the next week, Ms. V. suggested they close in prayer. At Samantha's nod of agreement, she began praying for Samantha, her family and their church, which would be going through a time of transition and healing.

When they were done, she was surprised to have Samantha come around her desk and give her a long hug. The action warmed her heart and brought moisture to her eyes.

"Thank you, Ms. V., for everything," Samantha said after releasing her.

"It's my joy and pleasure to help," Ms. V. said as she stood up and walked Samantha to the door. This was one of the times when she knew that God had designed her for this job. The gifts of discernment and wisdom He'd given her had not allowed Ms. V. to dismiss Samantha's change in behavior, but give the teen the time she needed to safe enough to let her guard down and share the cause of her pain. Ms. V. was extremely grateful for everyone's sakes. She served a sovereign God and He was faithful and just.

Chapter 14

For it is God who works in you to will and to act in order to fulfill his good purpose.
Philippians 2:13

"I'm a work in progress."

Ms. V.'s fingers wrapped around the doorknob just as the school bell rang, signaling the beginning of the lunch hour. She stepped into the hall after Samantha, turning to see Madison doing a little shuffle down the hallway towards them singing "God is a Good God," Ms. V. couldn't help answering in like manner "Yes He is." They both grinned at each other, not having to say another word.

They fell in step together, pausing and shifting every now and then to avoid doors being flung open and the students rushing around them as they made their way to the teacher's lounge.

Unlike the kinetic movement of the hall, the lounge was quiet. Most of the tables were still empty due to the earliness of the hour. The few teachers occupying seats were talking quietly amongst themselves, as if they were trying to preserve the serene atmosphere of the room.

Ms. V. set her purse down next to Madison's and was halfway to the refrigerator when she realized she hadn't placed her lunch in it that morning. She turned back, ready to apologize to Madison, when her gaze fell on the small feast her friend was spreading out on their table.

"What's all this?" Ms. V. asked, catching the rich scents of tomato sauce and sweet bread. Madison seemed to pull an endless supply of containers from her bag, and Ms. V.'s mouth began to water.

"I owed you lunch, remember? I told you yesterday that I was going to bring you something special." Madison said each word firmly, sparing Ms. V. only a quick glance. Ms. V. paused in her perusal of the containers, looking back up at Madison. She tried to think back to the conversation, but there was nothing to guide her. Usually she could pick any point in her day or week and recall any conversations she had with people, but at that moment it seemed as though the threads were missing.

She remembered waking up that morning, arriving at her office, speaking to Mr. Sanderson and Samantha. She even remembered the day before, but when she tried to recall the conversation with Madison things became fuzzy at best, and the more she tried to remember the more pressure she felt in her head. *It was one memory, and it was just about food.* She chided herself for getting worked up. It would probably come back to her later when she least expected it. She shook off the uneasy feeling, bringing a container of baked fish to her nose. The delicious scent made her stomach grumble, gaining Madison's attention. The women stared at each other, then burst out laughing.

"Come on. Sit down. I'll get the utensils," Madison said before stepping away. Ms. V. took a seat as she continued to breathe deeply. There was some of everything, fried chicken, meatballs, potato salad, bean salad, antipasto, tomato soup, grilled cheese, turkey sandwiches, raw broccoli, carrots, baby peppers and tomatoes, fresh fruit, sweet dinner rolls, cupcakes…it seemed to go on. How had Madison's bag held so much food? An even better question was who, was going to eat all of it?

Ms. V. looked up as the door to the lounge opened. In poured the rest of the teachers, as if they were all coming from one place. They filled the rest of the tables and the noise level rose. She caught more than one person eyeing the food at her table, but no one did more than smile at her when they met gazes. The door opened again, and this time Myra entered, followed immediately by Mr. McNeely.

Myra headed toward Ms. V., seemingly unaware of the man at her side. She pulled out the chair between Ms. V. and the one Madison's purse was resting in and sat down, smiling at Ms. V.

The gentleman stopped, looking from Myra to Ms.V. with confusion clouding his expression. Ms. V. opened her mouth to invite him to sit down, but Myra, who had begun to look over the containers on the table, shifted, knocking her knee against Ms. V.'s. The movement startled Ms. V. enough to pull her attention away from the man and back to Myra, who gave her a small shake of her head.

Hoping the man didn't catch the exchange, Ms. V. looked up at him with an overbright smile. "Mr. McNeely. How's your day going?" Mr. McNeely's gaze jumped from Myra and Ms. V. watched as his expression shifted to general courtesy.

"It's going well for a Wednesday. The closer we get to the end of the year, the harder it is to keep the students' attention, but I still have a few tricks up my sleeves."

"Good to hear, Mr. McNeely." Ms. V. replied then found she didn't have anything else to say. She glanced at Myra who was taking a whiff of the dinner rolls, acting oblivious to the conversation going on over her head. Ms. V. considered her behavior rude and had every intention of inviting Mr. McNeely to sit with them when Madison came back to the table.

Madison's expression went from bright to sardonic as she noticed Myra sitting between Ms. V. and her purse.

"Hi, Madison." Myra blurted out, sounding apologetic. "Do you mind if I sit here? I wanted to discuss something with Ms. V., and she told me it would be all right for me to sit with you for lunch." Indecision crossed Madison's face, but before she could speak, Myra continued.

"Mr. McNeely, it looks like Mr. Sanderson is trying to get your attention," Myra said. They all looked in the direction of Myra's gaze. Sure enough, Mr. Sanderson was waving in their direction, but Ms. V. was sure he was looking at Myra rather than Mr. McNeely.

"I think you should go over and see what he wants. We can talk later." Myra added the second sentence hastily. Mr. McNeely looked at all of them, his expression inscrutable.

"Sure," he said, looking down at Myra. "We'll talk later." He glanced at Ms. V. and Madison. "Ladies." Ms. V. nodded at Mr. McNeely, feeling both uncomfortable and baffled by the situation. As he left the table to head to Mr. Sanderson, confusion crossed Mr. Sanderson's features and he slowly lowered his hand.

"I don't understand it." Myra began. "It's like I just started working here. People are coming up to me in the office just to talk and the men are..." Myra glanced over at the other side of the lounge. "Everywhere." Myra sighed and Ms. V. pressed her lips together to keep from smiling. "They don't follow you two around like this and you are plenty nice."

Madison picked her purse up and walked to the seat on other side of Ms. V., handing Ms. V. the plate and eating utensils she'd retrieved. "They're used to us. We're nice all the time." Madison said matter-of-factly. Ms. V. threw her friend a look and Madison rolled her eyes before leaning forward to look around Ms. V. at Myra. "You'll get used to it."

Ms. V. continued to look pointedly at Madison and her friend sighed. "Why don't you go get yourself a plate," Madison said. "I can see now that I fixed entirely too much food for just me and Ms. V." She almost sounded sincere. Ms. V. smiled at her and patted her hand under the table in gratitude.

"Are you sure?" Myra asked. "I'm not intruding?" Ms. V. wanted to tell the woman to just accept Madison's invitation and leave well enough alone.

"No, You're not intruding, I bring food for just anyone," Madison said just under breath.

Ms. V. ignored the words and kept her thoughts to herself as she urged Myra out of her seat. "Go on. Get some. There's plenty, but we only have so much time for our lunch."

Myra's face broke out in a smile as she stood up. "Thank you. I'll be right back."

As soon as she was out of hearing range, Ms. V. turned to Madison. "Give the woman a break. Her father just died and she's feeling lost. It could be a lot worse. This could have caused her to be even more bitter, rather than open to change."

"First of all, that *was* me giving her a break. Second, I think it was because you didn't just let her stand in the middle of this room with egg on her face - like I would have - that caused her to see that she needed to change her ways." Madison shrugged. I'm a work in progress. You already know this. Just because I forgive her for the way she's treated everyone, especially you, I don't have to forget."

Ms. V. had to admit that Madison had a point. If nothing else, Madison was an honesty, loyal and caring friend. She had proved it time and time again. So, she let it go.

"This all smells so delicious," Ms. V. said, changing the subject "What do you think I should try first?" She grew excited again at the prospect of sampling some of everything on the table.

"We have tomato soup, grilled cheese sandwiches, fresh vegetables…" Madison started off, making Ms. V.'s mouth water once again. She looked up to see that Myra had gotten stopped by Betty Stubbing, the eleventh and twelfth-grade advance English teacher. Myra didn't look put off or anxious to get back to their table, so Ms. V. didn't feel the need to go rescue her.

"And mashed potatoes, apple sauce, graham crackers, chocolate milk, tea or these really refreshing ice chips if you'd prefer. There is also a Jell-o cup with fruit for dessert."

Ms. V. turned back to Madison, surprised by the last few items she'd named. Ms. V. hadn't noticed the Jell-o or applesauce, but when she looked down at the table, they were right in front of her.

"There's Salisbury steak and green beans," Madison said, placing a slice of meat and vegetables on her plate along with the potatoes. Ms. V. stared at them for a moment before looking at the table in front of her. The once container-filed table now had only a few bowls and cups. Was she dreaming? Her senses were all over the place. She was sure there was fish and chicken on the table a few minutes ago. She'd smelled them, along with the potato salad. Hadn't she?

Mrs. V. remembered Myra looking interested in the different foods laid out on the table earlier. She wondered if the woman had seen the same foods she had. She looked up to see if Myra was any closer to coming back to the table and noticed that she was now surrounded by three other teachers. It was going to be a while, but Ms. V. was happy Myra had been so readily embraced by the teaching staff. They had more than enough justification to ostracize her after her behavior for so long, but it almost seemed as if they had been waiting for her to have a moment of vulnerability. Not for a chance to pounce on her like handicapped prey, but to embrace her and give her comfort while she was open enough to receive it.

Ms. V. turned back to her meal, took a deep breath, and started cutting into her steak. Madison had made a beautiful gesture, and Ms. V. wasn't going to throw it away.

Twenty minutes later, Myra came back to the table with her plate and utensils. "That was crazy. I didn't mean to be gone for so long. Is there any food left?"

Madison slid a few quarter-filled containers to Myra across the smooth surface of the table. Ms. V. intercepted them and gently placed them before Myra. Ms. V. watched Myra eat in silence for a few minutes, noticing how peaceful the lounge was now that Myra had let go of her antagonistic attitude.

"Thank you for allowing me to eat lunch with you. I was afraid of how people would react to me today." Myra glanced up from her meal at Ms. V., giving her a sheepish smile. "Even after what you said and the morning visits from some of them, I wasn't sure if I would still be treated the same. I just wanted to let you know I appreciate you." Myra looked around Ms. V. to Madison. "You too, Madison. Thank you for sharing your lunch with me. You didn't have to."

Ms. V. was at a disadvantage since she couldn't see both their expressions without turning her head, but she chose to gauge her friend's reaction to the 'new' Myra.

"At least she didn't take it for granted," Madison mumbled before she leaned forward and gave Myra a small smile in return. "I don't know what I was thinking. Ms. V. eats like a very slow baby bird. You helped me out. I would have had to lug all of this back home," Madison said the words almost graciously.

Ms. V. didn't try to stop the smile forming on her lips. She was proud of her friend. Her heart was soft even though she tried to hide it.

"Tomorrow, dessert is on me," Myra offered. "What do you think of apple pie? There's this bakery down the street from my house, and they have the best Apple Brown Betty."

Ms. V.'s stomach pitched at the thought of another food with apples. "Cherry. I like cherry pie," Ms. V. said firmly.

"Really? I don't remember you liking cherry pie." Madison said.

"Yes, it has been my favorite for a long time," Ms. V. said with finality in her tone.

The table went quiet again when Myra went back to her food, but as teachers began to pack up and leave, quite a few stopped by their table to offer Myra their condolences and a word of kindness.

At one point, there was a small crowd around the table and Ms. V. was tempted to get up and give those around her more room, but Mr. McNeely stood behind her chair with a card in his hand. He reached out, only to be cut off by another teacher leaning in to offer her condolences and help with any arrangements Myra might need, since their cousin worked for a mortuary.

Again, Mr. McNeely tried to place his card in front of Myra, and again his path was blocked before he could set it down. It reminded Ms. V. of the day in the lounge when Myra had gone off on a tirade and Mr. McNeely had been forced to play a crude form of double-Dutch just to get to a spoon. Ms. v. smiled to herself.

Confident that Myra would be fine and feeling a little crowded by the people standing around, Ms. V. purposefully rose from her chair closest to Madison so she could exchange places with Mr. McNeely, giving him the space needed to deliver the card.

Madison joined her and Ms. V. rested a hand on Myra's shoulder as a form of goodbye. Myra glanced between her and Madison and smiled.

"Tomorrow," she said. "Cherry."

"Cherry," Ms. V. repeated before she and Madison left the room.

As they walked down the hall back to her room, Ms. V. thought about what had happened in the teacher's lounge, and how readily the group of teachers had opened their arms and offered support to Myra. It was only one of the reasons why she was proud of her employment at Center of Hope Academy. The open and compassionate nature of most of the faculty was uplifting.

"Okay, maybe she isn't so bad," Madison said, standing to her right.

Ms. V. glanced at her friend before smiling. "Maybe not.," she echoed as she stepped in front of her door.

"Hey, did you make up your mind on whether or not you wanted to go to the gospel concert on Friday evening? I've been holding the ticket for some time, waiting on your answer, but I need to know by the end of today, just in case I need to find someone else to give the ticket to."

Ms. V. turned to look at Madison. For the life of her, she couldn't remember any conversation about a gospel concert. She bit her lip at Madison's expression of open curiosity.

"Yes. Yes, I'll go. Do you mind giving me all the details again? I must not have been paying good enough attention the first time. I've had so much on my mind lately." Ms. V. rubbed her forehead, which seemed just a little warm. "I promise to give you my undivided attention this time, or if you want, you can write it down and give it to me at the end of the day."

Madison tipped her head to the side, studying Ms. V. "Sure, I don't mind, but it's not like you to be so forgetful. Are you feeling all right? You've been looking peculiar for the past few weeks."

Ms. V. considered how much to share with her friend about her episodes. She didn't want to worry her, only to find out she was suffering from a sinus or inner ear infection, both of which could account for her bouts of dizziness and fatigue. She would wait until after her doctor's appointment.

"I've been a little tired lately, but it is probably due to the heavier workload as it gets closer to the end of the school year. I haven't been sleeping well, but I think that will get better once school lets out." Ms. V. responded with a nonchalance she didn't feel.

"Okay," Madison said with concern written on her face. "You let me know if there's anything I can do."

"Yes, of course," Ms. V. replied. "The bell's about to ring and I have another session to get ready for. I'll see you later, okay?"

"Yeah, sure," Madison said. She paused a moment as if she wanted to say something, but smiled briefly and continued down the hall.

Ms. V. watched her friend for a moment before letting herself into her office.

Chapter 15

I will praise thee; for I am fearfully and wonderfully made: marvelous are thy works; and that my soul knoweth right well.
Psalms 139:14

"I am beautiful."

Ms. V. walked to her desk, trying to put her conversation with Madison and her much- dreaded upcoming doctor's appointment out of her mind. She needed to keep her head and spirit clear so she could listen, discern and advise her students as needed for the rest of the afternoon.

Over the last few weeks, she'd observed Porcha and her friends before and sometimes during the transition of classes. Ms. V. hadn't seen any obvious changes in the young lady's demeanor or actions, for the better or worse.

Ms. V. looked into Porcha's friend, Majestic's records to check if she was still enrolled in the Christian Academy. She noted that Majestic had selected Dr. Faerian as her counselor. Though they sometimes conferred with one another about students who wanted to change counselors or shared students who had conflicts with one another, Ms. V. rarely asked for or shared information with Dr. Faerian about the students they counseled.

She hesitated to approach Dr. Faerian about Majestic and her alleged pregnancy since the information came from another student. She decided to see if Porcha brought Majestic and her plight up again to determine if the young woman's situation warranted sharing with her counselor.

The firm knock on her door pulled Ms. V. from her thoughts. "Come in," she called out as she set Porcha's folder in her upper drawer, in case the visitor wasn't her student.

Porcha poked her head in the door then entered at Ms. V.'s beckoning gesture.

"Hi, Ms. V." Porcha's voice rang out with more confidence than Ms. V. could remember hearing before.

"Hello, Porcha." Ms. V. greeted, as Porcha closed the door and strolled across the room to her desk. She slid into the chair opposite Ms. V. and gave her a serene and peaceful smile. Ms. V. felt a weight lift off her spiritual shoulders and smiled back at the young lady.

"You are looking better than the last time we spoke. I take it things are going well for you?"

Porcha opened her mouth then closed it, pausing. "Um, yes and no, then yes again." She smiled sheepishly.

"Okay." Ms. V. made a show of looking at her watch but found her I.D. bracelet in its place. She blinked away the confusion, since she didn't want to lose focus, and glanced at the wall clock. "We better start then. We only have forty-five minutes. I will open us up in prayer and you can tell me about this see-saw you've been on."

Porcha giggled and nodded before bowing her head.

"Heavenly Father, the Great I Am. We come before you with humble hearts and hands lifted in surrender. I ask that your Holy Spirit guide this meeting. Let what needs to be focused on stay in the forefront of our memories. Search our hearts, sift through our emotions and allow Your truth to shine brightly. I thank you for what you have done in Porcha and her family's life. I thank you for what you are continuing to do. Thank you for Your peace, Your love, and the attention You continue to give us. We give you full reign of this session to do Your will. In Jesus, name. Amen."

Porcha lifted her head, her eyes shining as they met Ms. V.'s. She shifted in her seat and took a deep breath while Ms. V. settled back to listen.

"I think the last time I was in here I was trying to decide whether I was going to do what I thought it took to stay with Kevin, and my friend Majestic found out she was pregnant," Porcha reported.

Ms. V. inclined her head, thinking that was just the gist of what had been discussed, but it was obviously what Porcha was focused on. "That was some of it," she stated.

"Well, Majestic had a miscarriage, and though I'm kinda sad that a life was lost, I think it's for the best. She wasn't ready for a baby." Porcha sounded relieved. Ms. V. watched her even closer after the comment, wondering who may have been more relieved, Porcha or Majestic.

"I'm glad she's going to finish school with everyone else, but I wonder if she's really okay," Porcha said, seeming deep in thought as she spoke.

"Do you know if Majestic has talked to her counselor?" Ms. V. asked

"I think so, but he seemed to think it was a prayer answered in her favor and she should just be happy not to have to raise a child so early. Do you think she could talk to you if she continues to have questions about her body and whether or not this may happen again…you know later…way later…like when she's married?"

"Sure. I would be happy to, but I would have to make Dr. Farean aware that we talked."

"I don't think she would mind," Porcha responded before cocking her head to the side in thought. "Do you think abstinence is harder once you've had sex?"

Ms. V. took a breath before responding so that it looked as though she gave the answer, some thought when in fact it had been on the tip of her tongue as soon as Porcha finished the question.

"It depends. Everyone's experience is different, but I would say that it is usually harder to abstain once you've experienced anything known to be pleasurable."

Porcha nodded. "I thought so," she said, more to herself than to Ms. V., before looking back up. "Well, that is the good and the bad news." Porcha seemed to snap back into a lighter mood. "In *other* news, Kevin broke up with me." Ms. V. ran Porcha's words through her head again since the smile on the girl's lips didn't match her words.

"I take it this is a good thing?" Ms. V. phrased the thought as a question to invite an explanation.

"Not at first," Porcha said slowly, sounding preoccupied. "I was upset that he decided to go to college single after all the talk about how much he loved and cared for me, but when I remembered what I'd prayed to God about Kevin and our relationship, it all made sense. I also thought it was pretty awesome how God answered my prayer."

"What did you pray, if you don't mind me asking?" Ms. V. sat forward in her chair.

"I asked God to remove him from my life if he wasn't for me." Porcha's smile dimmed and she shrugged. "He wasn't for me."

Porcha blinked a few times and Ms. V. could see that she was trying to hold back tears. "I'm not sure what I'm more pleased about. God answering my prayer so quickly or Kevin listening to Him as I have been."

"Why do you say that? Did you not think Kevin listened to God?"

"Sometimes, but other times he seemed so headstrong about getting his way. I find it confusing that he could try so hard to get me to do something with him he knew was opposite of what God wanted, considering all of the times we had Bible study together."

"Why?" Ms. V. asked. "Was he not allowed flaws?"

"Yes. But he tempted me, and he knew it was wrong."

"What bothers you more, the fact that he invited you to do something you knew was a sin in the eyes of God or that you were tempted?" Ms. replied.

"As the priest of the home, isn't he supposed to guide by trusting in God?" Porcha asked as if already knowing the answer.

"Yes. As the priest of the home, once he learns what that is. Kevin is not a priest of anyone's home. He would have to commit himself before God and his wife to become the priest of the home. Right now, he is a teenager, like yourself, trying to listen to God more than your flesh. Sometimes you succeed, sometimes you don't." Ms. V. paused so that her words could be absorbed before continuing. "Don't lower Kevin in your eyes to justify what God decided was best for you. The decision God gave you wasn't just for your benefit, but for Kevin's as well."

Ms. V. watched as Porcha stared down at a point on her desk. Finally, she inhaled deeply. "I guess it was selfish to think that this was all about me."

"Yes, but the important thing is that it is also about you. God answered your prayer, and you were not only quiet enough to hear Him; you were mindful enough to ask Him in the first place." Ms. V. answered in all honesty.

Porcha's countenance lightened. "I did, didn't I." She smiled and Ms. V. found herself once again resisting the urge to shake her head.

"So, what's next?" Ms. V. asked.

"I'll make better choices on whom I spend my time with?"

"How are you going to do that?" Ms. V. asked

"I'm going to let God choose. It might take a while, but I've been thinking about what you said about me loving myself enough not to need the next guy I'm with to tell me I'm beautiful. I mean it will be nice to hear." Porcha shrugged. "But I won't need it because I'll already know."

"Good for you," Ms. V. said, feeling such a sense of pride at Porcha's realization that she repeated herself. "Good for you."

Porcha beamed at her. "Thank you, Ms. V. Thank you for never talking down to me and allowing me to come to this conclusion on my own."

Ms. V. nodded in acceptance of Porcha's shown gratitude.

"I was wondering something," Porcha said fidgeting with the shoulder strap of her purse.

"What is that?" Ms. V. asked.

"I was wondering if it would be all right if I prayed for you." Ms. V. stared at her for a moment, making sure she'd heard her correctly. No student, in all the years she'd worked there, had asked to pray for her.

"If you don't want me to, it' okay," Porcha said, backtracking.

157

"I think that is very thoughtful of you, but first I should ask if there is anything else you want to discuss."

Porcha looked up at the ceiling as if trying to conjure up a thought, but then looked back at Ms. V. and shook her head to the negative. "No. There's nothing else."

"Okay then, I'm all yours," Ms. V. said before lowering her lids without closing her eyes. She'd never close her eyes when in a session with a student, no matter the cause. It was her job to always be diligent.

Ms. V. heard Porcha inhale deeply before she began and was glad the young lady treated this moment seriously.

"Dear Lord. I thank you for being who you are in our lives. I thank you for the time and patience you have with each of us and using me to pray for your servant. I present Ms. V. before you. She is a hard worker and she really cares for children. Your children. I know it isn't as easy as it looks, but she is always ready to share a word of wisdom and advice, so I thank you for giving her that gift. She gives so much to all of us. She is a blessing and I thank you for giving her to us." Porcha paused for a few seconds before continuing and Ms. V. felt the shift in the air of the room.

"Father, I thank you for her warrior's spirit. She has been battling against the enemy for everyone for so long. Lord, give her the strength to finish what you had her begin. Let her have victory over the enemy and then I ask that you give her rest. A healing rest that will cause everything that is going wrong in her body to do its job correctly. Bless her mightily Lord. Give her green pastures to lay on and cool rivers to drink from. Restore her Lord; body, soul and spirit. In Jesus, name. Amen."

"Amen." Ms. V. repeated, her voice gruff with emotion. She swallowed a couple of times before attempting to speak. "Thank you, Porcha."

"You're welcome. Ms. V.," Porcha said, smiling softy before standing and giving Ms. V. a glimpse of the woman she would one day become.

"Porcha," Ms. V. said to stall the young lady.

"Yes, Ms. V.?" Porcha paused before turning towards the door. The light coming from the window hit her in such a way that it made her shimmer and glow, causing Ms. V. to blink a couple of times to see if she was imagining it.

"Continue to listen to God. He will never steer you wrong." Ms. V. said the words just in case Porcha questioned what God had her pray.

Porcha gave her a dazzling smile before nodding and turning to walk to the door. The shimmer staying around her even as she walked through the shadows of the room.

"Porcha." Ms. V. called out one more time, wanting to delay the young women's exit so she could continue to witness the tangible proof of God's anointing on her. Porcha turned to face her. "Have a wonderfully blessed summer, if I don't see you beforehand."

"You too, Ms. V.," Porcha said before opening the door and exiting the room.

Ms. V. leaned back in her chair and closed her eyes for a moment. The presence of the Lord was still heavy in the room, and she basked in the feeling of His essence being so intense upon her. She was reminded of something in that instance and she looked down at her arm to see that her watch was there, just as she remembered donning it that morning. She shook her head and closed her eyes again.

"Lord, I feel You here. Please restore my mind. I will lean on you, Lord. I will lean on you."

Chapter 16

Not by might, not by power, but by my spirit, saith the Lord of hosts.
Zechariah 4:6

"Not by my power or might, but by my Spirit."

Images began playing behind her eyelids. Pictures of students, past and present flickered across her line of sight like a reel of film. Every now and then, the reel would slow long enough for her to be able to make out a specific student, and she felt compelled to pray for them. The prayers ranged from physical healing to recovery of emotional trauma, and financial help, but each one drew more and more virtue from her until the weight of her weariness almost became too much to bear.

The reel sped up and slowed one last time, and Ms. V.'s eyes widened at the picture in front of her. She blinked, wanting to make sure she was seeing the picture clearly, then felt herself being pulled toward the huge field in the photo. She thought about struggling but was too tired. Something wasn't right. Normally when she was faced with the spiritual battlefield, she felt empowered and confident in God's presence and the Holy Spirit's authority that guided her. This time she only felt fear as she took her place on the muddied ground. It wasn't just her fear, it was fear from some of the children still lined up on the other side of the field. There was something more. There was a disconnect between her and the children; no eye contact, no recognition when their eyes moved her way, no movement toward her side of the line. Something over their heads caught her attention, and she looked up to see dark figures flying around in a chaotic manner. The children ducked and huddled together, looking around for whatever was causing the occasional breeze built up by the figures. It took only a moment for her to realize that the children couldn't see them.

A dark figure dipped low, catching one of the children off guard. The hem of its ragged and torn edges brushed up against the boy's shoulder and Ms. V. watched as his countenance changed. The boy stopped cowering and stood to his full height. He walked over to the girls that were huddled in a small circle with their arms wrapped around each other. As he approached them Ms. V. could see the aggression radiating around him like a green mist. She couldn't say how she knew what the mist meant. It was more instinct than knowledge that caused her to tense as the boy stopped next to the other teens who seemed to draw in on themselves.

His stance became intimidating as he leaned over them, anger contorting his features. Ms. V. yelled for him to stop but the sound of her voice came back to her ears in an odd manner, traveling no further than the length of her arm. She stepped forward in hopes of getting the boy's attention, but she hit an invisible barrier. She slapped her hands again the surface, which was warm to the touch, hoping to make enough noise to get any of the children's attention. She needed to let them know she was there; that there was no need to cower. They were children of God. They had the authority given to them in the name of Jesus Christ. She hit and punched at the wall, desperate to stop the boy who had begun to shove at one of the other teens. His aggression escalated as he began yelling at her.

Ms. V. couldn't make out what he was screaming but knew by his stance and the fear on the girl's face that it was threatening.

The girl began to cry, and Ms. V. watched as the dark figures' movements became sporadic and frenzied. The children huddling around the girl tried to soothe her, but she was beyond consoling. The more she cried the wilder the creatures flew until her sorrow emanated from her in gray waves. One of the creatures swooped down, getting close enough to pull the waves from her. Ms. V.'s stomach turned, and her heart dropped as she realized the creature was feeding off of her sorrow. She hit at the wall and screamed with renewed force, desperate to get someone's attention. She sobbed out her frustration, but her breath caught when the dark creatures turned her way.

Ms. V. quieted her soul on an inhale before closing her eyes and beginning to pray. She prayed for herself and for the knowledge of how to get the children away from the creatures. She also began praying for strength but was stopped, unable to utter the words. She exhaled and dug deep to find God's voice and heard a whisper pass through her mind. "Not by my power or might, but by my Spirit."

Ms. V. resisted the urge to place her hands on the wall and push again. *Not by my power...* She went over the words again and again, wondering why getting a clear thought through was like sifting through mud. *By my spirit.* Ms. V. got down on her knees, ignoring the dark figures that had begun to make their way toward her.

"Holy Spirit please guide me. There is confusion here. It's so deep. Please, shine your light on this place. Guide me and I will obediently follow you." Ms. V. bowed her head when the temptation to look up to gage the distance between herself and the creatures became nearly irresistible. She sought that place of peace, the place of worship and began humming while the lyrics sang through her head. *You are the Lord my God.* A sense of wellbeing flowed over her, resting on her back and shoulders and she felt shrouded. She rested and found strength in surrendering. She lowered herself even more, laying prostrate on the barren ground and giving herself over to the move of the Spirit.

There was a splintering sound all around her, followed by shattering glass and a forceful wind that would have sent her flying if she hadn't been laying on the ground. Her heart grew light at the thought that she had truly heard correctly. "Now go get the rest of my children," His voice said, and she opened her eyes.

***

Ms. V. blinked against the light in her office. Gone were the battlefield, the dark figures and the children. She looked around the room, trying to ground herself in reality. Ms. V. noticed that her breathing was shallow, and she forced herself to take deep breaths to calm her racing heart. Her ears picked up the sound of an alarm, but even as she strained to make out what it was, the sound stopped and was replaced with rhythmic beeping. Though the beeping calmed her after the sound of the alarm, she couldn't understand why she would be able to hear anything in her otherwise quiet room. She ran a trembling hand across her face as she tried to shake the prickly feeling running through her arms and legs. Her body was still in fight-or-flight mode, and it was taking more and more time for her to calm down after warring in the spirit.

She glanced up at the clock to see that half an hour had gone by. She had fallen asleep in the middle of a workday. The thought horrified her. What was wrong? Though she felt rested, she couldn't remember the last time she'd needed to nap in the middle of the day. It was a good thing no one had walked in.

Ms. V. stood up and walked over to her lounge area to pour herself a glass of water from a covered carafe. The cool liquid helped separate the fog that lingered from her dream. Instead of moving back to her desk right away, Ms. V. sat down on her couch and began praying.

Dear Lord, thank you for using me. You are the Lord my God. You are my strong tower and my place of refuge. Thank you for your wisdom and guidance. Thank you for your hand on me and these children. Continue to use me Lord and give me the wherewithal to do your will. Lord, I ask that you heal and save the boy in my dream. Touch his mind and heart, God. Deliver him, Father. Please give me the clarity to accomplish what you would have me to do. I seek your face, not your hand and I will always be your servant. In Jesus' name. Amen

Chapter 17

*And I will pray the Father, and he shall give you another Comforter,
that he may abide with you for ever.*
John 14:16

"It's scary moving across the country, meeting new people, starting
all over again in a new school by myself."

Glass in hand, she went back to her desk and picked up the file
for her next session. Jordan Green would arrive in ten minutes. Ms.
V. hoped the session she'd had with the Green twins weeks before
had given Jordan the courage to step out on her own and embrace
some new relationships. Time would only tell. Ms. V. couldn't
discern anything from her grades, since they'd remained as high as
they always were, but then again, that could be a sign that Jordan
had received her brother's advice during their last session.

She took another sip of water and decided to walk around her
office until Jordan arrived. She was almost relieved when the
knock came five minutes later.

Ms. V. sat behind her desk moving Jordan's folder to the top
drawer of her desk and called out for the person on the other side
of the door to come in. Jordan poked her head in, a hesitant smile
on her face.

"Are you ready for me, Ms. V.?" Jordan asked.

Ms. V. wanted to ask the teen if she had good news for her but
instead beckoned for Jordan to enter. "Yes, I am. I'm looking
forward to hearing about what you've been up to."

Jordan closed the door behind her. Her intelligent eyes looked bright and alive. Ms. V. could tell even by her gait that the teen had come out of her shell more.

Ms. V. opened them up in prayer once Jordan sat down then sat forward, giving the young lady all of her attention. "Have you made a decision about college?" Ms. V. asked when Jordan didn't jump in.

"Yes. I'm going to Luke University in the fall." Jordan's smile dimmed a little but there was determination in her eyes, and that let Ms. V. know that Jordan's focus was back on school and not solely on her brother and the health of her grandmother.

"I talked to mi abuela and she assured me that no matter what happened she would always be honest with me about her health," Jordan said. "That way I wouldn't have to worry so much about what I was missing while I was gone for months at a time." Ms. V. was unable to read her emotions.

"How do you feel about that?"

Jordan gave her a ghost of a smile. "It's something. I'm not completely sure she will keep up her side of the bargain, but Joel promised he would check in often and I believe him. Besides, I would know if he was hiding something from me. He has never been a good liar."

Ms. V. took in what Jordan was saying and watched the young lady. "What about you? Besides your reservations about your grandmother's health and being states away from your brother, are there any other concerns you have about going to school away from home?"

"Ms. V. I don't think we have enough time in this session to discuss them all. It's scary moving across the country, meeting new people, starting all over again in a new school by myself." Jordan shivered slightly.

"The only consolation is that there will be hundreds of other students that feel the same way I do," she continued. "I won't be alone in that way. It may help me find a friend or two. At least, that is what my mom says." Jordan finished quirking her mouth to the side.

"Do you believe her?" Ms. V. asked.

"Yes, but it's much easier said than done," Jordan replied.

"That is true." Ms. V. agreed. "How is your relationship with your brother going?"

Jordan sighed. "I miss him. I miss having him at arm's length or even within hearing distance, but I understand. If I can't cope with him being on the other side of the lunchroom, I won't make it with him being on the other side of the country." Jordan seemed to go into deep thought and Ms. V. waited, feeling as though Jordan was about to reveal something deeper.

"I just don't want him to forget me, you know? After seventeen years of being together—eighteen if you count the womb—I don't know how I would handle it if he went on with his life and forgot about me." Bowed her head.

"Do you think you could forget about him?" Ms. V. asked.

Jordan's head jerked up. "No. Of course not. I still feel him sometimes when I'm focused on something else, and I know he's either upset or concerned about something. He's a part of me."

"I don't believe it's much different for him. Your connection with him is not only one way. In fact, I would venture to say that with you being the one that is leaving, he is having some of his own concerns about you forgetting him."

"But I'm not leaving him. I'm going to school, and he wouldn't let me back out of it." Jordan's face was full of hurt and confusion.

Ms. V. reached out and patted the teen's hand. "He loves you. He wants you to be happy and have the best. Luke Divinity School of Medicine is definitely the best. It is a new school and new experiences, but it isn't a replacement for your life or family. It's merely a transition. There is no replacement for your relationship with your brother. You two have a special bond. I can tell just by how much you care for one another. It will take some adjusting and patience. He won't be there automatically when you call, and sometimes you won't be able to drop what you are doing to pick up a call from him. Professors frown on that sort of thing in the middle of their lectures, you know." Ms. V. added the last part for levity in hopes of relieving some of the tension from the room.

Jordan's misty eyes cleared, and she smiled softly. "You think so?"

"Yes," Ms. V. answered with all confidence. She was rewarded with a nod from Jordan. "How has it been since you and your brother decided to spend more time with your friends rather than with each other? I see your grades haven't suffered, so I'm hoping it means things are going well."

Jordan looked over Ms. V.'s shoulder for a moment then made eye contact with her. "I'm not as popular as Joel. I have a few friends, but I think they liked hanging with me for my brother's company more than mine." She sighed. "So, I have more time for my studies, but I'm hoping when I go to school that the girls will like me for me instead of how close they can get to my brother."

"Are all of them like that?" Ms. V. asked in concern.

"No. Shannon is cool. When we hang out it doesn't matter who's around, but she has younger siblings to take care of. Her mother recently died, and her father is raising them. She says he's a good dad and she knows he loves her and her brothers, but he's a little scattered sometimes. He forgets practices and playdates and she has to pick up the slack. She was going to go out of town for college and now she's staying here and going to a junior college the first two years so she can stay around the house longer. It feels almost uncomfortable when I bring up anything about going away to school, because I don't want to rub it in. It's just different now. She's more of a mom than a teenager." Jordan delivered the last sentence with a shrug.

"That has to be hard. Do you think she's afraid of you forgetting her once you leave?" Ms. V. asked and could tell by Jordan's stunned expression that she hadn't considered her friend's feelings.

"I wouldn't. She's my only true friend outside of Joel." Jordan proclaimed.

"Have you told her that?" Ms. V. asked.

Jordan's mouth closed and she looked slightly ashamed.

"I'm sure it will be fine. I know you have a lot going on in your mind about so many things. It's hard to see yourself through other people's eyes, but just remember that the key to any relationship is communication. You can't assume people are thinking or feeling a certain way or avoid a conversation in hopes it will go away. Since you and your brother are used to communicating on a lot of different levels, this may be a challenge, but I think you're up for it."

"Yes. Ms. V.," Jordan said, sounding thoughtful.

"Do you have any questions, Jordan? Anything at all?"

Jordan seemed surprised by her question, but relaxed when Ms. V. didn't press. "Um, not really. You gave me some things to think about though. How do you do that?"

"Lots and lots of practice," Ms. V. replied. Jordan laughed.

"I bet," she said before she sobered. "No. I don't have anything else, except to thank you for pushing Joel and me to put some distance between ourselves. I see after these few weeks, it would have been so much harder in August if we hadn't."

"My pleasure. I think you will be just fine, Jordan."

"Yes. I think so too." Jordan opened her mouth to say something else but a knock at the door had her shutting it.

"You were going to say something else?" Ms. V. prompted.

Jordan look back at the door, then to Ms. V. "I was going to say that Joel would be here soon, and I wanted to catch Shannon before fifth period was over so we could talk."

Ms. V. stared at Jordan for a moment. "You think that's Joel on the other side of the door?"

"I know it is," Jordan said. "He's early, as usual." Another knock came, and Ms. V. became curious.

"Are you sure there isn't anything else on your mind you wish to discuss?"

"I'm sure," Jordan said without hesitation.

"Okay." Ms. V. nodded. "Come in!" she said loudly and watched as Joel entered her room.

Jordan turned to him and then back to Ms. V. and lifted one brow as if to say, "Told you." Jordan collected her things and got up from her chair. "See you at graduation?"

Ms. V. smiled. "See you at the graduation ceremony."

She watched as Jordan placed her purse on her shoulder, turned and began walking towards her brother. No words were exchanged as they passed one another, but they high-fived then low-fived each other. The move on a whole looked practiced to perfection. The only thing ruining their air of coolness was the small giggle that escaped Jordan as she continued to the door, which elicited a grin from Joel. Yeah, they were all right.

As Jordan slipped out of the door, Joel took her place in the seat in front of Ms. V. He sat there for a few seconds, his back ramrod straight, before looking back at the now-closed door.

Ms. V. wondered what he was thinking and asked as much.

Joel's shoulder's slumped as he turned back to face her. "I'm not sure Jordan should go away to college."

Well, this was a 180-degree turn. Joel had all but ordered Jordan to go to Luke University. She waited, sure a comment so profound would be followed by an explanation. When after a few seconds it wasn't forthcoming, Ms. V. raised her eyebrows at him. "You start our session with a statement like that and follow it up with silence? I didn't take you for a dramatic person."

"I'm just trying to get my thoughts together so I can tell you why I feel that way," Joel said sheepishly.

"Very well, I will wait."

"Do you know Kevin Marsh?"

"Yes." She didn't share more.

Joel watched her for a moment then, if it were possible, his shoulders drooped even more. "Are you his counselor?" He asked.

"I think you know I can't share that information with you, but you can talk. In fact, I welcome it."

Joel was quiet for a long time before speaking. "Kevin used to be a decent guy. He was actually somewhat of a nerd during our first year here. We hung out some since we both were into mechanics a few years ago. He played around. You know, joked a lot, but I think it was to hide some of the challenges he had with dealing with his home life." Ms. V. remained quiet and still to keep from drawing Joel's attention away from his story. She didn't like the way this was going. First Porcha then Joel. What had happened since her exit counseling session with Kevin?

"Kevin changed when he joined the football team. It was gradual, but the more he hung out with them and the more problems his family had, the less he reminded me of the Kevin I spent hours with in the mechanic's workshop our freshman year." Joel rubbed his hands against the legs of his jeans and went quiet and stayed that way so long Ms. V. was concerned his time would run out before he really got to the point.

"You are that concerned about Kevin?" She asked as a prompt to bring him back to the present conversation. Joel blinked a couple of times before she saw him focus back on her.

"No. Well, yes, but he isn't my main concern; just boys like him." He blew out a breath as if the confession had taken a lot off his shoulders. Ms. V. thought she knew where he was going with his comment but had learned long ago not to make assumptions.

"I'm going to need you to elaborate, Joel," she said when he went quiet again.

He focused on her once again. "My sister is going to be hours and miles away, surrounded by boys like Kevin. I won't be able to reach her easily if she finds herself in trouble. I've always looked out for her and now…Just seeing what Kevin has become over the last few weeks and knowing he's going to be going away to college to do whatever, brought it home to me that Jordan will be around boys like him."

Ms. V. understood the anxiety that went along with separation and didn't doubt that Joel was experiencing some of that at this very moment. She also knew Joel cared very deeply for his sister and was honestly concerned for her. If she didn't intervene though, it could get out of hand.

"Would you say you know your sister well?" Ms. V. asked Joel.

"Um, yes."

"Better than most?"

"Yes," Joel replied, beginning to give her his undivided attention.

"Does your sister sneak out at night or hang out with questionable people?" Ms. V. asked.

"No," Joel said, drawing out the word and looking at Ms. V. as if she'd lost her mind.

"Does she have a lot of boyfriends?"

"She hasn't had any, not for lack of guys trying." He hmphed and Ms. V. got the distinct feeling that he may have played a role in dissuading a boy or two from approaching her.

"Do you think your sister has good judgment?" Ms. V. went on.

"Yes, of course," Joel answered and she thought she saw it dawn on him what he was saying and where she was leading him.

"I think the best thing you can do for yourself and your sister right now is to trust her and trust what you know about her. She may not be as knowledgeable about the minds of men, but you can always warn her if you think it will make you feel better about her wellbeing." When Joel opened his mouth Ms. V. pointed her finger at him. "Warn… Joel, not order or tell, just give brotherly insight that might help her see certain people with questionable motives coming."

Joel stared at her for a moment. "Is that being dishonest?"

"Are you planning on telling her lies, or sharing more of the bad about people's intentions than the good?" Ms. V. asked, leveling him with a stare of her own.

"No," he said. "I just want her to be safe."

"Then approach her with that in mind. You already gave me your answers about how well she can take care of herself when you are in the room or when you are hours away." Ms. V said before leaning back. "And if I'm not mistaken, you are already keeping an eye on your abuela."

Joel blew out a breath. "Yes, I am," he said then chuckled. "I can either juggle a whole bunch of stuff and people or I can give it to God."

Ms. V. was only mildly surprise by his statement after their last session. "Well, that is completely up to you."

He gave her a ghost of a smile. "My mom said the same thing."

"Your mother sounds like a very wise woman," Ms. V. quipped.

The smile Joel gave with his next words was real and bigger. "Yes. She is. Jordan is a lot like her." His smile faded a little. "I'm going to miss her." He lifted moist eyes to meet hers. He rolled his eyes right before he wiped at them. He shrugged his shoulders. "I was so busy trying to prepare Jordan for her time away from me and the family I didn't consider how I would feel."

Ms. V. pushed the box of tissue toward him. He gave her a sidelong glance then pulled one from the box.

"Good for you, Joel," Ms. V. said sincerely. Joel's eyes snapped up from gazing at the surface of her desk to her face. "This is only one of many transitions you will be making in life. Check in with yourself. You matter a great deal to the people who love you. If you want to continue to take care of others, you have to take care of yourself first, which means staying in touch with your feelings and continuing to express them, even if you just share them with yourself."

He watched her for a moment then nodded once.

"Is there anything you're concerned about regarding your schooling?" Ms. V. asked.

Joel answered with little hesitation. "No, not really. I know some of what to expect and what I don't know I find exciting and adventurous. I'm looking forward to it."

Ms. V. watched to see if he truly meant what he said, and he seemed sincere, so she took him at his word. "Is there anything else you want to talk about?"

"Um, no. I think that was all I had on my mind."

Ms. V. watched him for a few seconds before nodding. "Okay, then. Mr. Green, let's close out this session with prayer." She watched as he inhaled deeply then bowed his head.

"Dear Heavenly Father, I give you thanks for your precious son Joel. I thank you for giving him the heart of a protector. I ask that you continue to cover him with your grace and mercy. Holy Spirit, comfort, lead and guide him through this next phase in his life. Give him the strength to let go of those things that are held easier in Your hands, Lord. Give him peace regarding his family and friends and continue to direct him on his path to help others. These things we pray in Jesus' name. Amen.

When Joel looked up, his eyes were bright but only a little moist. "Thank you for everything, Ms. V."

"You're welcome, Joel," she said looking up at him as he slipped on his backpack.

"I will never forget you," Joel said before turning towards the door.

His words caught Ms. V. off guard. There were still a couple of weeks left in the semester, along with the graduation ceremony, yet Joel had said them as if he wouldn't see her again. She watched the door close behind him, feeling a bit disquieted.

Ms. V. glanced at the clock. She was relieved to see it was close to the end of the school day. As encouraging as her sessions were, they were still taxing. She filed away the folder, then placed tabs on the files owned by students who had already gone through their exit sessions. By the time she lifted her purse out of the bottom drawer, the school's dismissal bell was ringing. She wasn't even going to pretend it wouldn't be an early night. She would stop by the store to pick up a ready-to-go meal, reheat it when she got home, eat and take a soothing bath before slipping between her sheets. She could hear them calling even as she closed and locked her office door behind her.

Chapter 18

For the weapons of our warfare are not carnal, but mighty through God to the pulling down of strong holds;
2 Corinthians 10:4

"Wield your sword, warrior."

When Ms. V. stepped out of the dense thicket onto the edge of the field, the battle had already begun. She looked around at the soldiers standing with her along the sidelines, helmets on, breastplates secured, belts cinched, shoes ready, shields up and swords poised. She didn't remember having this much help before, and the thought that others were praying and warring alongside her came to her with clarity and comforting peace. They could do this together, get the last of the children and secure the rest of the souls for God. She glanced up at the sky looking for a parting in the clouds or a shift in the wind; something to let her know when to step up.

The mud being kicked up by those battling in the middle of the field made it hard to discern who was friend or foe. The light shining from within the fighters was dimmed by the caked-on muck covering them from head to toe, but every now and then a sparkle of light would peek through, momentarily blinding their foe and they would get the advantage. During one such instance, the demon let out a scream of frustration and charged blindly at a soldier, but he stood still until the dark force grew near enough to touch, then he sidestepped and spoke as the demon passed.

"Jesus," he said.

The dark figure seemed to stumble, but he didn't go down flat. He skidded so that he ended up impaling himself upon the sword of the soldier behind his fellow guardsman, in the kneeling position.

Sword after sword whistled through the air, the sound, like a chant, reaching her ears seconds later. *"Behold, I give unto you power to tread on serpents and scorpions, and over all of the power of the enemy: and nothing shall by any means hurt you."[1]* It reverberated through her and the soldiers by her side. Ms. V. glanced down at her sword, reading the inscription on the blade out loud once again,

"For though we walk in the flesh, we do not war after the flesh: For the weapons of our warfare are not carnal, but mighty through God to the pulling down of strongholds;" The words strengthened and comforted her, reminding her of her lineage and the promise God gave her.

Ms. V. felt more than saw the restlessness of those on the sidelines, waiting for her to give the command to join the battle, but she, too, was waiting. There was one child she hadn't spotted yet, and she wouldn't leave the field until he was safely back on their side. She scanned the opposite side for the children and found some huddled in groups and others scattered, traipsing back and forth, watching the sky. She looked up in time to see a dark figure dive toward a child. The girl sat down at the last second, narrowly avoiding whatever plot or scheme the dark figure had planned. Ms. V. wasn't sure if the child could see what the other children couldn't, or if it was just perfect timing.

Ms. V. continued to scan the children, looking for the boy she'd seen earlier. She told herself she would not leave him to the fate of becoming one of those creatures. She concentrated on each face until she found him. She almost didn't recognize him; his body was twisted in such a way that each step he took looked painful. His movements were stiff, and when he came close to another child his face would morph into that of one of the dark figures hovering above them. Her heartbeat doubled in rhythm and she took hold of every ounce of determination rising up in her, gripping the sword in her hand even tighter and yelling a battle cry so fierce she wouldn't have been surprised if it cracked the sky. *"What then shall we say to these things?"*[2]

The answering cry of the beings around her vibrated through her, *"If God be for us, who can be against us?"*[3] It acted as the ignition to a motor and galvanized her into motion.

The race was on. She knew once those on the sidelines joined in the battle it wouldn't be long before the forces of evil were beat back. Her focus was on shining a light on the dark figures hovering over the children and drawing the boy out from the influence of the demons before it was too late. She ran as if her life depended on it across the field, moving too quickly for her shoes to sink into the muck. Her heart gave an uncomfortable pang in her chest, but she pressed on, following a path through the battling crowd as if it had been drawn out specifically for her. It brought her right up to the edge and she planted herself there, wielding her sword, listening to its call as it beckoned the children to her. *"Ye are of God, little children, and have overcome them: because greater is he that is in you, than he that is in the world."*[4]

She swung it over her head in an arc, listening to it sing out. *"Submit yourselves therefore to God. Resist! Resist! Resist the devil, and he will flee from you."*[5] She noticed she'd caught the boy's attention as well, and the dark figures' movements became chaotic. She watched him as she raised her sword again, letting it speak for her as it cut through the dense fog lowering over the field. *"No weapon that is formed against thee shall prosper; and every tongue that shall rise against thee in judgment thou shalt condemn. This is the heritage of the servants of the LORD, and their righteousness is of me, saith the LORD."*[6]

The children stepped over the line one at a time onto the battlefield, led by the young girl Ms. V. had noticed earlier. They gathered around, not moving more than a foot away from her. The figures screeched louder, tumbling and whirling about, making it hard for Ms. V. to see if the last child, the one now disfigured, was moving forward or standing still.

Ms. V. felt the urgency coursing through her very being. Time was short. This was her last battle. The tempo of it beat in her heart, sang in the blood flowing through her veins, and whispered under her breath. This would be her last chance and she knew she would give everything she had to light the way to the truth for that last child shrouded in darkness.

Battle-weary soldiers emerged from the fog, taking children's hands to guide them through the dense haze to the other side of the field. Ms. V. was grateful she could concentrate on the one left. She lifted her sword, knowing from the stiffness in her shoulders she only had enough energy for a few more attempts at drawing him out. She brought it down hard against the ground, hearing its voice echo along the surface. *"Verily I say unto you, Whatsoever ye shall bind on earth shall be bound in heaven: and whatsoever ye shall loose on earth shall be loosed in heaven."*[7]

Sweat trickled down her face as she took in huge gulps of air. She needed to keep going. Not one would be sacrificed. Not one would be lost. Ms. V. lifted the sword again, turning herself in a circle and using her body's movement to carry the sword through the air. *"Be not overcome of evil but overcome evil with good."*[8]

When the sword came to a stop, Ms. V. looked up. In front of her was the boy. Her heart leaped with joy and she waited for him to come forward, but he stopped, hesitating as he caught sight of his reflection in her armor. "No." her heart cried out. "God, please let him see himself as You see him. Let him see the beautiful young man who will change the world just by being obedient to You. Show him the authority and strength he can have in you."

"Wield your sword, warrior."

She set the sword to her right and inhaled deeply. She bent and lifted the sword as she straightened, taking it over her head to the left. It barely touched the ground on her other side before she bent and straightened again, repeating the action over and over. She created an archway that would give the boy safe passage if he chose to come forward, all the while listening to the sword speak.

"And ye shall know the truth, and the truth shall make you free."[9]

One dark force separated from the pack and charged at her to keep the boy from advancing. The tip of her sword severed the demon in half on its downward path.

"The LORD shall cause thine enemies that rise up against thee to be smitten before thy face: they shall come out against thee one way, and flee before thee seven ways."[10]

Up the sword went again with light both leading and following its course.

"These things I have spoken unto you, that in me ye might have peace. In the world ye shall have tribulation: but be of good cheer; I have overcome the world."[11]

"The thief cometh not, but for to steal, and to kill, and to destroy: I am come that they might have life, and that they might have it more abundantly."[12]

The sword bounced off the ground with a clang and ascended again.

"But the Lord is faithful, who shall establish you, and keep you from evil."[13]

And on and on she went, feeling the boy move closer and closer to the edge until he raised his foot as she brought the sword up and over one more time.

The sword swung.

"He that dwelleth in the secret place of the Most High shall abide under the shadow of the Almighty. I will say of the LORD, He is my refuge and my fortress: my God; in him will I trust."[14]

The boy fell into her and she rejoiced. She could feel him wrap the one good arm around her as he pressed his face against the shoulder of her breastplate. She could feel the virtue leaving her body as the light from her armor illuminated him from the inside out. She turned them around and was relieved to see the mist part, then fade, clearing the same path back to the other side of the field.

The boy's other arm, now healed, wrapped around her and it was all she could do to guide him across the now quiet battlefield. She dragged her sword behind her, unwilling to let it go, hoping it would sing one more time, for her.

By the time they reached the other side she was spent, and he was keeping *her* up. His body was restored to its full strength and he was standing upright. God was faithful. He had seen her through until the last child was delivered.

***

The Choice is Yours

You've come to a crossroads in this story. This book has the added element of an alternate ending, giving you the opportunity to choose the fate of Ms. V's journey.

If you wish to take a more spiritual journey with Ms. V., skip to Chapter 23 on page 223

If you wish to experience Ms. V.'s journey on a natural path continue reading.

***

Ms. V. fell to her knees, completely spent. Her virtue was gone. A small hand appeared in her line of sight. She followed the hand up the arm to see the person who was offering her help and frowned. Merissa Dokes? She wasn't supposed to be here. She'd already prayed her through, hadn't she? There was an inner glow that got brighter as Ms. V. watched until she had to cover her eyes.

This time, when she felt the familiar tugging in her center, Ms. V. was ready. She had fought the good fight. She had finished her course and kept the faith. She had brought the last soul home and now she could rest.

Ms. V. turned to see familiar brown eyes also watching her. She smiled at Kevin. She felt as if she were on a precipice. She could decide to take Merissa Doke's hand or let the feeling in her center take her. The time her indecision cost made the choice for her, and she closed her eyes just before she was pulled from the battlefield.

Chapter 19

KJV: "Nor height, nor depth, nor any other creature, shall be able to separate us from the love of God, which is in Christ Jesus our Lord."
Romans 8:39

"You are loved."

Madison breathed a sigh of relief as she walked through the doors. That was one thing she could always count on when coming into this place - the air conditioning would be on. On the other hand, if she came in too early, she could also count on a stronger scent of disinfectant in the air. Madison wondered idly, with all of the chemicals, if the janitor's sense of smell was still intact. She shifted the plant in her hands and settled her purse strap more securely on her shoulder.

She kept her head down as she looked at the same white tile she saw every time she walked down these halls. She wondered if it was due to her hesitance to meet anyone else's eyes, or her reluctance to be in this place altogether. She never knew what she would get when she hazarded to glance up into the eyes of passersby.

Giving herself a short pep talk and squaring her shoulders, she forced herself to glance up in time to meet the somber eyes of a child. She cringed inwardly but tipped her lips up in a smile that was not returned by the child. She brought her gaze up higher to meet the eyes of the mother holding on to the child's hand. Her eyes mirrored the sadness in the child's, but she gave Madison a shadow of a smile in return. Madison hadn't remembered seeing them before, and wondered briefly at their sadness. She said a silent prayer for them as they passed each other. There was so much pain and sadness in the world. It was as if an invisible war was being waged...and she felt like she had just witnessed some of the collateral damage.

Madison shivered and picked up her pace as she rounded the corner to an even more familiar hallway. She found that if she looked like she was in a hurry, people tended to avoid niceties and pleasantries. Madison just wasn't in the mood today. She had awakened from a deep sleep that morning in a sweat with the remnants of a dream that had shaken her to the core, and she felt compelled to see her friend.

She finally arrived at her destination. She inhaled, pasting a huge smile on her face before giving the door a swift knock as she always did, then entered her best friend's room.

"Hello Sunshine. Blessings be upon you," Madison sing-songed as she made her way across the room to the once-organized display of cards, mementos and flowers, and tried to find a place for the thriving plant in her hand.

"If you ever doubted how much you are loved and respected, I think this display should dispel that. I don't know too many people who would receive constant gifts for a month, let alone three months." She spoke over her shoulder without taking her eyes off of the display. "You are truly blessed."

Madison slowly perused the gifts to see if anything had been added since her last visit, and to see if there were any flowers that needed to be transferred from their vase to the trash under the table. Finding a small space between a card and stuffed bear that had accompanied a bouquet of flowers that had long since been discarded, she set the cellophane-covered plant holder in place.

"Perfect." She adjusted the plant and stood back to take in the overall view. "What do you think? I think it's in exactly the right place. It looks like I will have to pack up some of these so you can take them home with you." Madison took a couple more steps back before turning to her friend.

"So, the plant is from Myra," she continued. "Who for some reason thought it urgent that I give it to you." Oh." She exclaimed before stepping close. "Let me help a sistah out." She smoothed a hair back in place that had escaped her friend's ponytail. "That's better."

She pulled an envelope from her purse and held it up. "This is from Kevin Marsh. Yes, I know. Kevin Marsh of all people. Let me read it. I'm dying to see what he told you." She opened the envelope and pulled out a card with a picture of a lavender field. There was gold embossed lettering at the top that she read out loud, "'It's the Little Things That Make All the Difference.' Mmm. I wonder what that means." Madison opened the card. A piece of paper slipped to the floor and she bent down to pick it up. It looked like a poem. Interesting.

Madison located the chair behind her and sat down. "Okay. Let's see what we have here." She placed the piece of paper behind the card and continued to read what was on the inside. "There are people and works of nature that we see every day. We walk by them, taking little notice until they make a huge impression on our lives." Madison paused briefly and lifted her eyebrows at her friend before continuing. "You are one of those big impressions.

Signed, Kevin Marsh. Wow," Madison exclaimed before switching the piece of paper to the front of the card.

"It looks like a poem," Madison informed her friend as she looked more carefully over the paper. "'Dear Ms. V.' is the title.

"You have been a part of my academic career since I began at Center of Hope.

The way you spoke to me; a counselor who cared, helped me cope.

Your eyes seemed to be everywhere without me noticing it.

And yet you treated me like everyone, not judging me one bit.

I and my friends are happy to have you as our counselor.

It is true because your gentle voice and firm hand make you very popular

I know when I graduate, because of you, I will leave with a different point of view

It can be summed up with one phrase you gave, "God's blessings be upon you."

God's blessings be upon you too, Ms. V.

~ Kevin." Madison smiled and lifted moist eyes to her friend. "That was actually really nice. A rhyming poem? Who knew Kevin had it in him?" She shrugged. "Well, I guess by this poem, you did.

"I don't know how you do it. I think all of the students that you counsel adore you. Well, as they should. 'Cause I adore you." She leaned back slightly, placing a hand on her chest. What's your secret?" she asked, leaning forward.

Madison's focus was diverted as the door opened.

"Hi, Dr. Newton," she said.

"Ms. Marino. I'm glad I caught you here. I have some news I think you're going to like."

Madison's heartbeat picked up in anticipation. She refrained from asking her friend if she'd heard him, knowing it might sound odd to someone else, even though it had become commonplace over the last three months. She leaned back from her friend's bedside, waiting for the good news from Beatrice's – or Ms. V.'s – doctor.

Madison looked around the hospital room. It was the same as it had been the day before and the day before that. The fact that there was no change in the appearance of the room both soothed and agitated her. The tile was the same. The lighting that competed with the sun streaming through the one window in the room was the same. The sound of the clock echoing in rhythm with the beeping of the monitor ringing in the hollowness of the room was the same.

Each day she prayed something would be different. Was this that day? The motionlessness of her best friend weighed on her, though she tried hard to carry only upbeat and healing thoughts with her into the room.

It had been hard. She missed her friend. She missed the extraordinary woman of God who could quote and apply scripture to any situation. She missed the vibrancy of the woman who rarely sat still, who was ready for just about anything even after a full day of counseling children. She wondered if Ms. V. knew just how many students – past and present – had visited her. Madison believed Ms. V. could hear her and those that came to sit and talk to her. She didn't know how. There was no outward sign that Ms. V. was listening, but Madison could feel her friend's awareness. She hadn't tried to explain or convince anyone of it. She just knew what she knew.

"Like I said, I might have some good news for you," Dr. Newton began again, pulling Madison from her thoughts. "Things are still a little tentative due to the unprecedented nature of our findings over the last few months."

Madison focused on the doctor, hoping today wouldn't be like the last three months or that wretched day in November when Madison walked into Ms. V.'s office to meet her before them going together to their weekly dinner. She'd called out to her twice before walking further into the room and spotted her foot sticking out from behind her desk.

Madison blinked away the memory and forced herself to stay in the present with the doctor standing in front of her.

"Toward the end of yesterday, your friend's monitor was showing some odd readings. I don't have to tell you how grave things looked after her third week here with very little brain activity. You also know that over the last month the activity has gradually changed for the good until yesterday." He shook his head as if perplexed before continuing. "We aren't really sure how to read the numbers we have been getting on Ms. Vacherchesse's brain activity, but I choose to take it as a positive sign."

Madison's hand came to her chest instinctively, as if the action could keep her heart from beating through her breastbone. What was he saying? Hadn't he said she might like what he had to say? Was Ms. V.'s brain activity no longer showing a gradual improvement? Had she taken a turn for the worse? Madison glanced over at her friend, trying to see if she had missed something vital that could be noticed in her friend's appearance, but there was nothing she could point out.

"There is still so much we don't know when it comes to brain injuries, but I always took it as a good sign that Ms. Vacherchesse dreamed."

Madison was startled by his statement. "Dreamed. She dreams?"

"Yes, we started picking up activity as well as noticed that her eyes would move back and forth – a sign of being in a R.E.M. cycle – during the early mornings," he said matter of matter-of-factly. "Since last evening Ms. Vacha...Vacherchesse.'s vitals have been fluctuating. At first, I was concerned that her body might be giving out. We see that in patients who have been in a coma for an extensive amount of time. Their vitals rise as if the body is giving one last push then everything drops and the organs fail. As I monitored Ms. Vera. . . Miss Vacherchesse through the night—" Madison interrupted him.

"Don't hurt yourself. That's why we all call her Ms. V. You have my permission to do the same."

"Well, ah, thank you," he said slowly, clearly having been caught off guard. Then he continued. "I noticed that the dips didn't last long, and the recovery brought her vitals up higher than they were before the dip. Since I honestly have never seen anything like it, I can only go with an optimistic theory.

"When I came in today, her vitals and brain activity were up thirty percent from yesterday. If I am right, I believe your friend is on her way to regaining consciousness."

"Really? Are you sure? How long will it take?" She opened her mouth to ask another question, but the doctor held up his hands in surrender to stop her.

"We aren't sure yet, but so far all of the tests look promising. I have been communicating with a number of neurological specialists since she came in and sharing her medical timeline with them, and they are almost as baffled as I am. None of them have seen anything to parallel the swift change in your friend. One of them went as far as to say it was nothing short of a miracle for her to continue to regain the type of brain activity we've seen in the last forty-eight hours."

He sighed as if the admission had taken something out of him. "If I were completely honest, I would say that we are in uncharted territory. In the beginning, all signs pointed to a much less desired outcome." Dr. Newton puffed up, pasting a smile on his face. "In spite of all of that, if everything continues as it is, and there is no sudden decline without recovery, I'm thinking we should start to see signs of her waking up over the next week. We will also be taking her breathing tube out tomorrow morning since it looks like she can now breathe on her own."

Madison thought over his words. She could be looking into her friend's big, brown, and oh- so-wise eyes within a week. It was indeed good news.

"I am telling you this because you are here almost every day, so if you see any obvious changes in her appearance or behavior, I ask that you get a nurse's attention as soon as possible."

Madison started nodding even before he finished his sentence. "Yes, of course."

"Very good." Dr. Newton gestured over to the display. "It's rare for a person who has been in a coma for her length of time to still receive this number of gifts. She must really be loved."

Madison followed his gaze to the table then turned back to him. "Yes. She is very much loved and missed." Madison responded.

"She's a school counselor, right?" Dr. Newton asked as he walked closer to one of the monitors.

"Yes," Madison replied, as she watched his movements with more interest than before. Her friend might wake up in a week. It seemed like some wonderful dream. Unlike the one she had the night before of Beatrice walking up to her, seeming weary from some great battle. She was dressed in mud encrusted-armor, her gait slow and slightly staggered. It was almost as if she were appearing through a fog. Madison watched her approach, waiting for her to say anything.

"Have you seen my sword?" Bea asked, a frown marring her features.

"What?"

"My sword. I lost it on the battlefield. I need it. I can't fight without it." Bea stepped up to Madison, grabbing her arms. "Where's my sword!"

Madison had awakened with the sound of Beatrice yelling in her head and an urgency in her heart to see her friend.

"I really liked my counselor as well," the doctor said, once again taking her away from her thoughts. "He was able to provoke thought with one sentence. It used to get me how he was able to do so much in one thirty-minute session. I think I will always remember him."

Dr. Newton walked over to the computer in the corner and started typing. Madison nodded and looked at Ms. V's unconscious form but didn't respond to his statement.

"I would love for you to wake up," she said to her friend, in earnest. "Not just for me, but for all of the people who have sent symbols of their love, support and encouragement. You are loved and blessed, Beatrice,"

Chapter 20

But, beloved, be not ignorant of this one thing, that one day is with the Lord as a thousand years, and a thousand years as one day.
II Peter 3:8

It is a day full of potential.

Ms. V. woke up slowly, unlike any of the other mornings after she had warred in the spirit, she struggled to open her eyes, but was relieved to see that it was still dark out. She closed her eyes again, gaining enough consciousness to wonder why her bedroom smelled so sterile before sinking back into a deep and hopefully restoring sleep.

Once again, Ms. V. had awakened without her alarm clock going off, a little bit in a panic. It took a moment for the grogginess to leave her, but she felt surprisingly energetic. She stood up slowly, and, feeling a little stiffness, she began her stretching exercises after praying. She went through the rest of her morning routine and left the house with more than enough time to take the slow way to school.

She was parking her car in the parking lot when an overwhelming sense of déjà vu came over her. She watched the children walking into the school building for a few moments, and noticed something odd about their clothing. Sure, they were in uniform, but some of the girl's accessories looked familiar. She looked down at her own blouse and skirt, and they looked very much like something she had worn the day before, but she had retrieved them from the part of the closet where her clean clothes were. Her I.D. bracelet was also on her wrist, but for once she felt it was meant to be there. She shook her head and dismissed the thought. She gathered up her keys and exited her car with her belongings.

Ms. V. took her time walking from the parking lot to the school building. She paused a few times trying to work out odd sounds that were incongruent with her surroundings. One moment birds were chirping in the trees surrounding the property, and the next moment she could hear what sounded like footsteps in an enclosed room. She turned around once but no one was behind her. She took a few more steps, but when she heard the beeping of a machine, she stopped again. What was going on? She glanced up at the sky, wondering if it would give her a clue to what was happening to her. It was blue and clear, except for one white cloud. She didn't know why, but the cloud brought her comfort. After a couple more seconds, the position made her dizzy, so she put her head down and made her way into the building, trying to remember when her doctor's appointment was again.

"Good morning, Ms. V. Blessings be upon you," Myra called out as Ms. V. stepped into the administrative office to collect her messages. It took her by surprise that Myra would greet her using her own phrase, then had to smile to herself. No one could own a blessing.

"And you as well, Myra. How is your morning?"

"It's good. I can't complain. Well, I could, but I'm trying to focus on the positive." Myra got up from her seat and walked up to the counter separating them. "I wanted to tell you that Mary Parker invited me to her church's Bible study Wednesday night, and I loved it. I'm going back next Wednesday. Her pastor is good at breaking things down, and he takes questions. Did you know you could ask questions in church? That's a new one on me. Anyway…" She turned back to her desk for a second before facing Ms. V. with a cellophane-wrapped plant. Myra placed it on the counter and pushed it toward Ms. V.

"I know I've said thank you before with the flowers, but I wanted to get you something that would last a little longer. You may never know how much you changed my life with your kindness, but I am truly grateful for you seeing past my pain." Myra stopped and shrugged then pushed the plant a little further. "Just thank you for being you. That's all."

Ms. V. took the plant, noticing that the last of the woman's admission had embarrassed her and Ms. V. didn't want to cause a scene.

"*Thank you,* Myra. That is more than kind of you. I love it," Ms. V. watched Myra beam at her words.

"You're welcome," Myra answered, before turning back to her desk and sitting down.

Skillfully dismissed, Ms. V. repositioned the plant in her hand, not removing the smile plastered to her face. She turned to her box and removed a purple envelope the size of a greeting card. She looked at the front of it. It just said, "Ms. V." She pulled the rest of the messages from her cubby hole and walked out of the Administrative office.

The walk through the halls was another exercise in focusing on reality. The smell was different. There was more of an antiseptic scent in the air, with less of the lemon fragrance she was used to. Plus, there was the intermittent sound of a ticking clock, which she surreptitiously looked for as she continued to her door.

She noticed that her walk to her office took longer than normal as she was hailed with a barrage of greetings and smiles from the students walking past her.

"Morning Ms. V.," Samantha said, and before she could fully respond another student yelled.

"What up, Ms. V. How's your morning?"

"Thank you. It's good."

"Hi, Ms. V."

"Hey Ms. V.

"Hello, hello, hi.," she replied over and over again until she was almost at her door.

"Good morning, Ms. V.," Porcha Grant greeted in passing.

"Good morning, Porcha. God's blessings be upon you," she returned.

"And to you," Porcha replied, her smile growing wider before she went back to talking to the friend she was walking with.

Ms. V. stopped at her door and slid her key into the lock. She jumped in surprise when a hand came into view, knocking on her door. She looked up into the smiling face of Mr. Sanderson.

"Good morning, Ms. V."

"Good morning, Mr. Sanderson. How are you doing?"

"You know, Ms. V. It is a day full of potential," Mr. Sanderson said.

Ms. V. was a little surprised by his optimistic reply but didn't comment on it. Instead, she looked him square in the eye and nodded.

He smiled over at her before shifting his stance. "God's blessings be upon you," he said before walking off. She followed him with her eyes until she lost him in the crowd of students in the hall.

She opened her door, smiling broadly and shaking her head. After closing the door again, Ms. V. walked to her lounge area and deposited the plant on the coffee table that held the bear. Then she proceeded to her desk, put her purse away and sifted through her messages until she got to the purple envelope.

A knock brought her head up, and she watched her best friend stuck her head in the door. "Good morning!"

"Good morning." Ms. V. returned.

"All clear?"

"Uh huh."

Madison came in and pushed the door closed behind her. She walked up to Ms. V.'s desk.

"What're you up to?"

"I got this card..." Ms. V. began.

"Who's it from?" Madison asked, interrupting her sentence.

"I'm not sure. I just picked it up."

"May I?" Madison held her hand out for the card.

Ms. V. didn't know why, but she handed over the card and leaned back to watch and listen as Madison opened the envelope and looked inside the card to find out who it was from.

"This is from Kevin Marsh," she said, lifting incredulous eyes to meet Ms. V.'s.

"Wow."

"Yes, I know. Kevin Marsh of all people. Let me read it. I'm dying to see what he told you." Madison read the cover of the card out loud., "'It's the Little Things That Make All the Difference. Mmm. I wonder what that means." Madison opened the card again.

A piece of paper slipped to the floor, and she bent down to pick it up.

Ms. V. watched as Madison located the chair behind her and sat down. "Okay. Let's see what we have here." She placed the piece of paper behind the card and continued to read what was on the inside of the card. Meanwhile, Ms. V. closed her eyes to take in the words Madison read.

"There are people and works of nature that we see every day. We walk by them, taking little notice until they make a huge impression on our lives." Madison paused briefly and Ms. V. opened her eyes to see Madison lift her eyebrows at her before continuing. She smiled and continued to listen.

"You are one of those big impressions. Signed, Kevin Marsh. Wow!" Madison exclaimed before shifting the piece of paper in front of the card.

"It looks like there's a poem," Madison informed her as she looked more carefully over the paper. 'Dear Ms. V.,' is the title."

As Madison read the poem, Ms. V.'s eyes warmed and watered. Kevin hadn't been her easiest student, but she knew he had the capacity for so much love, compassion and greatness. He would be okay. He would be okay.

Madison finished the poem, smiled and lifted moist eyes to her. "That was actually really nice. A rhyming poem? Who knew Kevin had it in him?" She shrugged. "Well, I guess by this poem, you did."

Ms. V. nodded and smiled.

"So, this evening. You. Me. Thursday dinner." Madison made her declaration as she stood up and handed Ms. V. back her card.

"Yes," Ms. V. replied, both amused and pleased to have something to look forward to. She had completely forgotten that it was Thursday.

"Good. I will come back here after school and we can go together."

"What about your car?" Ms. V. asked.

"It's in the shop," Madison said, as she started to make her way to the door.

"What would you have done if I told you I didn't feel like going to dinner?" Ms. V. asked, raising her voice slightly.

"I would have asked you to take me home," Madison replied, still moving toward the door.

"What if I told you I had a date?"

Madison stopped as she reached the door. She turned back to Ms. V. and gave her a look that said, *Really*. "I will see you after the last class."

"It is possible." Ms. V. called out.

"Yes, but after the disaster that was your marriage, and finally breaking free from your ex-husband fifteen years ago, I would want to know much more about any man you would even consider taking a cup of coffee from, let alone having a date with." Madison gave her a stern but protective look before walking out the door.

"There *is* that," Mrs. V. said, to the empty room. She stared at the card for a moment before setting it aside. She would put it with the plant and other presents. She opened her calendar to see who she was going to have exit sessions with that day. There was one person on the schedule. Merissa Dokes.

Ms. V. remembered the girl from earlier in the semester. They had only been able to have two sessions due to the student's poor health. She'd sent Merissa a few notes throughout the year but hoped they would at least be able to have an exit session. It would be nice to catch up.

Ms. V. took the rest of the morning to organize and file away all of the student's folders she'd had exit sessions with. It took longer than it should have with her bouts of disjointedness. There were often times where she felt as if she were in two places at once. It was hard to describe, but sometimes she would hear things or even smell things that had no business being in her room. There was the smell of graham crackers and apple sauce that also brought on a sense of déjà vu. At one point she laid her head back in her chair to relieve a ringing in her ears and the room tilted, causing her to nearly fall out of her seat. *Something was wrong.*

Ms. V. stayed in her room and laid on her couch during lunch. She would double-check to see if Merissa was in school that day. She should have done it sooner because if Merissa were absent, she could have had Madison take her home or to the emergency during their lunch. Home. Home would be better. No need to jump the gun when she had an upcoming appointment with her doctor.

Ms. V. opened her eyes and stared up at an unfamiliar ceiling. She blinked a few times, knowing she was seeing things on top of the sound and smells coming to her throughout the day. Was she having a waking dream? With that thought in mind, she began to concentrate on what she was seeing. White cardboard tiled ceiling with the holes that looked like a hole puncher went to town. There was a light somewhere. It illuminated most of the room, leaving the corners in the shadows. She tried to turn her head, but it wouldn't move, so she relied on her senses of smell and hearing to get more information about her surroundings. There was definitely a clock, and even though she couldn't see it, she could hear it. The same with whatever was beeping…Was she in a hospital? Who was in there? Who was she supposed to pray for? The rhythm of the beeping sped up, which caused her to wonder if the person was in some type of pain or distress.

"Sssh. Ssssh. God is with you, dear one. There's no need to be anxious. Father, please touch and heal this bedridden person. Please give them peace as you restore their, mind, body and emotions. Make them whole, Dear Lord."

Her prayer was cut off by an intense pressure on her chest and she clutched at it, squeezing her eyes closed in the process. Was the person having a heart attack?

Ms. V. woke up in her office on the couch, clutching her chest. Was *she* having a heart attack? The pressure eased some and she took in a gulping breath. This wasn't good. She rolled off of the couch and tried to stand to her feet. Her legs felt like Jell-O but they stayed under her until she reached her desk, where she promptly fell to her knees. The pain in her chest came back with a vengeance and it was all she could do to crawl to the side of her desk the phone was on.

Once the pain eased to a bearable pressure, she reached for the phone. The receiver felt like it weighed fifteen pounds and she barely removed it from its cradle. She tried to dial a number, but the next pain took her to the ground. She curled into the fetal position to try and find relief. She would have tried any position at the moment if it meant the elephant on her chest would step off.

The pain intensified, and she would have told anyone who asked her that someone had reached inside of her rib cage and was squeezing her heart. She tried to take a breath, but it stalled and tears came to her eyes. After a few seconds, the edges of her vision grew hazy and dark. She glanced at the clock and was surprised to see that hours had passed while she was on the couch. Her friend would be there to meet her soon. All she had to do was hold on. Just hold on.

As the darkness closed in around her the sounds and smells of the hospital grew more prominent, and with her last moment of consciousness, she realized who she'd been praying for in the hospital bed. It was herself.

Chapter 21

O LORD, how great are thy works! and thy thoughts are very deep.
Psalm 92:5

...all of that work and progress was a figment of her imagination.

Ms. V. woke up slowly. She held her breath for a moment, afraid the debilitating pain would return. She relaxed some when the pain didn't come. Maybe it had passed, and she could get up and have Madison take her to the hospital by car instead of ambulance. She took another cautious breath and when it only caused the briefest of pain, she decided rolling over might just work.

She tensed to move, but nothing happened. She took stock of her body and found that she was already on her back. Oh. Well then, she could just sit up. She tried to open her eyes to make sure she hadn't rolled under the desk. The process took so much strength she became anxious. *Why was it taking so much energy just to open her eyes?*

She finally opened them the barest bit, but it was enough to see that she wasn't in her schoolroom. The room did look familiar though. The beeping came to her in the haze of everything, and the picture that was her reality began to solidify. She was in the hospital. How had she gotten to the hospital? Had Madison found her? She would have to apologize – if her friend was still talking to her.

The sound of a door opening caught her attention and she waited for whoever came through it to walk into her line of sight, since moving her heavy head was nearly impossible. The footsteps stopped a few feet from the door, and she heard what sounded like typing. Still, she waited patiently for the person to move closer. When what seemed like hours passed, though she knew it was only a couple of minutes, her eyes began to get tired and she was afraid she would fall back to sleep before the person discovered that she was awake.

"Hello?" She rasped, alarmed at the roughened whisper that left her lips. The typing stopped and she exhaled in relief and hope that the person had heard her. She thought about lifting a hand, but the movement of her forefinger was all she could handle. It wasn't needed, though, because the footsteps started again, bringing a woman in scrubs into her field of vision.

The nurse peered at her and stepped to the right of her bed. She took her hand and squeezed it. Ms. V. summoned the last of her strength and squeezed back.

"Wonderful! You're awake. I'm Cara, your nurse. Can you open your eyes or squeeze my hand again? Was that you speaking?"

Ms. V. tried to hold on to the nurse's voice but was too exhausted to do any of the things she'd asked for. Maybe if she slept for a few minutes she could regain some strength.

The next time Ms. V. woke up she didn't have as hard a time opening her eyes. It felt early, like morning. She had no clue why. From the natural light in the room, it could just as easily be evening. She closed her eyes in prayer.

"Thank you for waking me, Father. Thank you for another day. I will strive to obey you so that I have more to give you. Amen."

She dozed but kept an ear out for a sound other than the clock. Why would a hospital room have such a loud clock? When the door opened, she waited before slowly opened her eyes again. This time the person didn't stop at the computer. They walked right to the side of her bed, took her hand and squeezed it gently. The next moment a screaming Madison leaned into her line of sight. Ms. V. wince at the assault on her ears and blinked at her.

Oh my! Oh my gosh!" Madison cupped her hands over her mouth. "Oh, my gawd!" She did a weird little hop before running over to the other side of the bed. She reached for a remote-looking device that had been resting on the edge of Ms. V's bed. She pressed a button over and over again, all the while smiling at Ms. V.

"You had me scared there for a moment, but I knew. I knew you were going to pull through. I..." She closed her mouth and Ms. V. wondered what she was going to say. Instead of continuing her sentence, Madison did the little hopping thing again as though she had too much energy to contain it. Then she stopped and just stared at her.

"Good morning beautiful," Madison said. "Welcome back."

It was so good to see her friend smiling at her, she couldn't stop the tears if she tried.

"Oh, don't cry. It will get in your hair and on your pillow." Madison moved away and came back with a tissue. She began to dab at the edges of Ms. V.'s eyes. "You don't want a wet pillow. They are not at all comfortable."

Ms. V. worked at building enough moisture in her mouth to answer her friend without pain. Suddenly her throat was on fire. "Water?" Her voice made her sound like a frog that just woke up.

"Of course. You must be parched." Madison let go of her hand and poured her a cup of water. She placed a straw in the cup and led the straw to Ms. V.'s mouth. She was grateful for the small dignity. She pulled at the water through the straw and it felt like cool silk sliding down her raw throat.

"I'm sorry," Ms. V. said when Madison took away the straw. Madison gave her an odd look.

"For what?"

"For the scare."

Madison's smile vanished, and her throat worked before she attempted to speak. "Forgiven," Madison said before taking back Ms. V.'s hand. "Just don't do it again."

"Deal." Ms. V. croaked and Madison gave her another sip of water.

The door to her room opened and she heard footsteps. They were medium-weight, but heavier than the nurse's, who came in earlier. A middle-aged man who looked to be of Indian descent came forward with a smile of his own.

"Good morning. I'm Dr. Newton. How are you feeling?"

Ms. V. search for a one-word answer that would suffice. "Awake."

"That you are. Do you mind if I check you out while I ask you a few questions?"

"No." She croaked.

"Do you think you can press your way through them?" he asked, as he shined a penlight in her eyes. "I know your throat is probably pretty raw right now." He pulled her chin down as a signal to open her mouth. She complied and waited for him to finish examining the back of her mouth and throat.

"Why raw?" she asked.

The doctor exchanged glances with Madison before looking back at her. "How about you answer my questions, then I will answer yours." He felt around her neck before stepping back.

Ms. V. gave him what she thought was a nod, but wasn't sure her head really moved.

Something must have happened though, because the doctor began his questions.

"Can you tell me your name?"

"Beatrice Vacherchesse."

She could tell he wanted to cringe at the sound her voice made pronouncing her name.

"And do you know where you are?"

"Hospital," she said and groaned.

"We're almost done. Do you know why you're here?"

Ms. V. remembered the excruciating pain in her chest that took her to the floor in her office.

"Heart attack?"

The doctor paused at her response. "Um, no, actually. You suffered a stroke, which put pressure on an already-weak blood vessel in the right side of your frontal lobe."

"Chest hurts," Ms. V. said, wanting an explanation for the severe pressure and pain she'd recently gone through.

"Just one more question," the doctor said, holding up his forefinger. "Do you know what the date is?"

"End of April? Just finished exit sessions for students."

Ms. V. notice the way both Madison and Dr. Newton went still. Once again, Dr. Newton looked at Madison then back at her.

"What?" Ms. V asked, hating to be left in the dark.

"Sorry, Ms. Vacha…Vacherchess," he said butchering her name with his accent.

"Ms. V."

"Ah, yes. I've heard that a time or two from your friend. Ms. V. If you had to guess, how long do you believe you've been out – as you put it?"

"Three – four days?"

She watched his face go blank in response to her answer. It was like shutters came over his features. He looked up and over to her left where she assumed her monitors were, since that was where the nurse had looked earlier as well.

"I'm going to tell you something, but I need you to try and stay calm."

This doctor's bedside manner needed help. Even she knew that you never told someone to stay calm because then they would question their need to stay calm and grow anxious, just as she was doing now.

Madison squeezed her hand and Ms. V. turned her focus on her. "It's fine. You're okay now."

She was. She was awake. That was a lot, considering. "Yes," she agreed.

"Ms. V., you suffered a stroke and hemorrhaging in your brain on November seventeenth of last year. Due to the trauma to your brain, the loss of blood, and the surgery needed to relieve some of the pressure, we had to put you in a coma, but when it was time for you to wake up, you didn't regain consciousness. Not until yesterday, when you woke up for a few minutes. You've been in a coma for three months."

Ms. V. couldn't wrap her head around what he was saying. She had just gone through two semesters of counseling with students and this doctor was telling her she, in essence, had dreamed the months after November? How was that possible? She was there every day. The students were there. There may have been some days that drifted together, but that was normal after doing the same profession for so many years in a row. This just didn't make sense.

"It was so real," she said.

"I'm sure," Dr. Newton said. "The mind is still a place science has very few answers for. You, for one, are a source of great curiosity for us. You are an exception to many of our case studies, but I can't say that I'm unhappy about that because you are here. You, Ms. V. are a miracle."

She didn't know how to make him understand what she was feeling; the interaction and experiences that she had with the students, staff and her friends just couldn't be the result of a dream.

She focused on the doctor's eyes and held his gaze for a few seconds before speaking. "I was there. Talked to the students." Her throat burned with her intensity. "Heard birds sing, ate lunch with the staff." She shifted her gaze to Madison's. "We all talked and prayed with Myra and she changed. She gave me a plant."

Madison's eyes widened.

"Yes," Ms. V. said, to reiterate her point, then thought about it. Three months ago, she would have thought Myra's change could only be something she dreamed up, and her heart dropped in despair. If what the doctor said was true, all of that work and progress was a figment of her imagination. Ms. V. felt the heaviness of that realization land on her and it made her incredibly tired. She closed her eyes to give herself a few minutes to reconcile what she knew to be, with the reality of that moment. *God. What did you do?*

"Beatrice?" The odd tone in her friend's voice had Ms. V. opening her eyes.

"We can talk about this more later because I can see you're exhausted. Myra did send you a plant."

If anyone could hear Ms. V.'s mind, they would have heard something akin to a needle scratching a vinyl record. "What?"

"Myra gave me a plant for you last week. She left a card with it. I can read it to you if you like, but from what I recall, she said that she was thankful for your kindness, that it changed her life? Something like that. She was happy you were you."

Ms. V. didn't know what to believe anymore. She let go of the breath she'd taken and closed her eyes again. At that moment it was all too much, but when Madison's hand released hers, she felt an urgency to relay something to Madison, so she summoned the strength to open her eyes again.

"Madison."

"Yes, beautiful. I'm here." Madison answered, coming back to her side.

"Thank you," Ms. V. said before giving in to the tiredness pulling at her.

Madison's chuckle was all she heard before the darkness claimed her.

Chapter 22

For I know the thoughts that I think toward you, saith the LORD, thoughts of peace, and not of evil, to give you an expected end.
Jeremiah 29:11

Miracles just like her.

This time Ms. V. woke to a shuffling sound. She couldn't discern whether it was paper or clothing. Maybe it was the curtains in her room moving against the window. She was sure she'd closed the window the night before though. Sensing the light before she opened her eyes, she squinted as she turned to see just how late it was, but there was no clock, no nightstand, no window. Fear gripped her before the memories all came rushing back. She was in the hospital.

"Good morning, Ms. V."

Ms. V. turned her head to see Dr. Newton standing at the edge of her bed.

"Morning." She responded before trying to clear her throat. The pain was still there, but it had dulled somewhat.

He gave her a gentle smile before sifting through some paperwork.

It had been papers she'd heard. Well, at least she'd gotten that correct.

"I must say that you continue to astound me," said the doctor. "I have never seen someone recover as quickly as you have been doing. From the tests we've run, I've been able to surmise that you've only lost some mobility in your left hand."

Her sword hand. Was that why she'd lost her sword on the field? Images of her battling demons came to her in a rush, swiftly stealing her breath. *That was her?*

"But that can be helped with rehabilitation," Dr. Newton said, pulling her away from her thoughts. "You are a medical marvel, but I want to advise you against doing too much too soon. You have been through a traumatic ordeal and your body needs rest. If I could have kept you in the ICU longer, I would have, but there was really no medical reason for me to delay moving you to our rehabilitation wing." Dr. Newton gave her a warning look she didn't understand. She didn't think she'd expressed an impatience to get out of the ICU, or even leave the hospital, for that matter.

"Did I do wrong?" she asked.

Dr. Newton seemed surprised by her question, then his features eased into a smile. "You don't know."

"Know what?" she asked confused by his words and reactions.

"You've had students and staff trying to get in to see you for the last three days. I was sure your friend would have told you. The nurse's staff got tired of turning them away, so they didn't resist Dr. Johnson's orders to have you moved since you are awake, cognitive and responding well to tests and the medication."

Since she took good care of herself at home, eating right and exercising consistently, she didn't expect less than a good report, but then she couldn't brag because she was in the hospital due to a stroke she could have avoided if she'd been more diligent about making and keeping her doctor's appointments. Had she made an appointment? It was hard trying to reconcile her reality with everything she had dreamed.

"I didn't know," Ms. V. said more to herself.

"Well, you seem to have a huge fan base and I don't blame them, but I want you to promise me that you will try to hold it back to three visitors a day, and if you are feeling tired, you will say something right away."

Ms. V. gave him her most solemn expression. "I will try."

Dr. Newton gave her a reluctant smile. "I guess that will have to do. I will be back to check on you before I leave for the day. Don't hesitate to have me paged if you start to experience dizziness, nausea or trouble forming or keeping thoughts, okay?" He ended his sentence by giving her a pointed look, which she felt she couldn't deny. She needed to incorporate that look into her counseling sessions.

"I will. I promise."

Dr. Newton nodded and walked out of the room, and it was then that she began to take in her new surroundings. She hadn't realized that she was in a whole different room. She would keep that information to herself. She was looking forward to seeing some of the students and staff that Dr. Newton was talking about.

***

A few hours later Ms. V. finished a lunch of chicken broth, apple sauce and lime Jell-O. Each bite tasted and felt familiar. *Huh.* Was it really possible that she had dreamed everything and that those dreams were influenced by her current environment? Still, that didn't explain the counseling sessions and coinciding gifts. Kevin Marsh and his poem came to mind. From what Madison had shared yesterday, he had visited a couple of times, as had Samantha Royce. Once by herself and then again with her father, who had prayed for Ms. V.

She was contemplating the situation when Madison walked in.

"I have a surprise for you," Madison said as she came closer, a bright smile plastered on her face. Ms. V. smiled back but was surprised when Madison presented her with a dark blouse.

"You have company, I thought you would want to put this on."

"From what the doctor and you've already told me, I have had many visitors."

"Yes, but you're awake now." Madison waving the blouse at her. "It's big enough to fit over your gown and from the looks of it, the hairstyle I gave you yesterday is holding up."

Ms. V. might have been miffed at all of the attention at any other time, but truthfully, she was grateful her friend had her back.

Madison drew the blouse on over Ms. V.'s hospital gown, then left the room, promising to be right back.

A minute later Ms. V. watched as students and staff filed in until there were ten people in her room. *Surely, they were breaking some type of hospital rule,* she thought to herself.

"Okay, we have to do this quickly before a nurse comes in here and shows us all out," Madison said in a stage whisper, excitement dripping from her words.

Ms. V. looked at the smiling faces made up of students and staff and felt her heart swell. She wondered how they had gotten past the nurse's station, then waved it off. She smiled and felt her chin wabble a little, she was so moved by this gesture. As she took in their features, she noticed that they looked a little older than she remembered, lending credence to her doctor's and Madison's claim that she had been in a coma for months instead of days.

"All of you get detention for breaking hospital rules," she said in her frog-like voice. She watched as some of the startled expressions at the sound of her voice and probably the fact that she made a joke, morphed into smiles and light laughter. It also seemed to give the line of people the permission they needed to break formation.

Dr. Sanderson approached her first, coming to the side of the bed and leaning in to make it easier for her to see and hear him. "Hello, Ms. V. It's good to see you awake," he said. "I've been praying for you. I got you a little something." He handed her a small wrapped box. She took it and held it to her chest.

"Thank you. How's your sister doing?" she asked automatically.

Mr. Sanderson gave her an odd look. She's doing well. Very well." He answered after a brief pause, though he looked surprised by the question.

"Cancer-free?" she elaborated as quietly as she could, just in case there was something else he was thinking of. He frowned as if confused, but nodded.

"Yes. Yes, she is. Thank you for asking," he replied, looking baffled, but before they could speak more Madison jumped in.

"Do you want me to hold that for you?" Madison's hand was extended out for the box Ms. V. was holding, Ms. V. shook her head and laid the box at her side.

"I'll keep it, please," she said, and her friend backed away. Ms. V. looked back at Mr. Sanderson. Thank you for coming and for the gift."

"I just want you to continue to heal," he murmured as he started to back away.

"I will," she said with as much confidence as she could muster.

Porcha stepped forward with a wrapped package as well, in the shape of a book. She handed it to Ms. V. who gave Porcha her most radiant smile.

"Hi, Ms. V. I'm glad you're awake. I've missed you." Porcha lent her a tremulous smile, which did nothing to hide the tears brewing in her eyes.

Ms. V. opened her free hand as a gesture for Porcha to take it. "How are you and Jesus doing?" Porcha gasped and covered her mouth. Ms. V. watched as the tears spilled over but when Porcha removed her hand she was smiling.

"We're good."

"Wonderful," Ms. V. exclaimed and squeezed the young woman's hand before letting go.

"I love you, Ms. V.," Porcha said, just before she pulled her hand from Ms. V's.

"I love you too."

Samantha Royce exchanged places with Porcha. She was dressed in a T-shirt and jeans, but they were her size. Ms. V.'s heart grew a few more centimeters in her chest.

"Nice outfit." Ms. V. mumbled with a smile. Samantha looked down at what she was wearing then back up at Ms. V. with a small crease between her brows. Ms. V. ignored the look, knowing they didn't have long.

"Are you ushering in the Holy Spirit with your music?" Samantha's eyes widened, but she didn't miss a beat with her breathy response.

"Yeah."

"Good."

"I'll play for you some time." Samantha offered. It was Ms. V's turn to be surprised, but she only nodded, as she was momentarily unable to talk around the lump in her throat. Samantha smiled and stepped back so Jordan and Joel could take her place at Ms. V.'s side.

"Well, well." Ms. V. adjusted her head to take both of the twins in. "Luke Divinity School and San Diego have no clue what's in store for them." Joel and Jordan exchanged glances before Joel looked back at Ms. V.

"How did you? How did you know?" Joel asked.

"We talked about it." Ms. V. reminded him.

"No. We didn't. You were already in here when we made the decision." Joel confirmed.

Ms. V. tried to sum up what he was saying with what she knew to be true and the room spun for a moment, making her dizzy. She closed her eyes and took a few breaths, hoping the feeling of disorientation would fade quickly.

"Are you all right?" Madison's voice was close to her ear.

"Yes. Just a little light-headedness," Ms. V. replied. When she opened her eyes a few moments later she was happy to see that the room and its occupants were straight and standing still.

Joel and Jordan had moved away and in their place was Myra. She had a tentative smile on her face. Ms. V. could sense her wariness and reached out to clasp her hand.

"How's the staff treating you?" Ms. V. didn't miss the stunned expression that passed over Myra's features and wanted to roll her eyes. *Not this woman, too!*

"They are treating me well."

"Good. And how is church?" Ms. V. asked and watched as Myra pressed her lips together before taking a deep breath.

"You know don't you," Myra said as she squeezed Ms. V.'s hand. "You know everything."

"Well, I don't know about everything…" Ms. V. started but was interrupted.

"You know about my dad?" Myra asked with sheen in her eyes.

"Of his transition? Yes." Ms. V. confirmed Myra's question with solemnity, and Myra smiled through her tears. She nodded and squeezed again. Myra opened her mouth again but was cut off by the sound of the door opening.

A nurse walked in and stopped short. Ms. V. watched as she took in all of the people in the room and knew the visit was over.

"How did you all get in here?"

"We walked," Porcha responded innocently and Ms. V. heard a snicker in Joel and Jordan's vicinity. The nurse looked at Porcha to see if she was being rude but must have surmised that Porcha was just trying to be helpful.

"Well then you all can just walk back out of here. We have a limit on visitors, and it looks like she has reached her quota for the day."

The students and staff started toward the door, but Ms. V. stopped them. "Thank you all for coming. I don't think any of this is a coincidence, but I consider it a gift to know you are doing well. God's blessings continue to be upon you." After that, she had to rest from the effort to make sure she expressed just how grateful she was. She resisted closing her eyes so that she could meet each person's gaze, and smiled back at everyone as they exited.

"Won't He do it?" Samantha asked, pointing at Ms. V.

"Yes, He will!" Joel and Jordan answered in unison as they stepped over the threshold.

Madison remained by her side, and the nurse gave her a pointed look.

"I'll be back tomorrow," Madison said as she gathered her belongings.

"I'll be here," Ms. V. replied jokingly, but Madison stopped what she was doing.

"Yes, you will, and I can't tell you how grateful I am that you will be. I've missed you very, very much my friend." Madison's expression was serious, and it occurred to Ms. V. that the time Madison had come into her office crying over a friend, she had been crying over her.

Ms. V. wasn't sure how God had walked her through these people's lives while she was laying in this bed, but one thing she did know, He was with her, prompting her to pray for herself and others. It was a humbling experience and one that confirmed even more that her life, her job and the prayer influenced by her relationship with God, helped create environments for miracles.

Miracles just like her.

***Continue reading for the alternate ending to this story.
***

Chapter 23: Alternate Ending

[b] Thus says the LORD to you: 'Do not be afraid nor dismayed because of this great multitude, for the battle is not yours, but God's.
2 Chronicles 20:15

She had brought the last soul home and now she could rest.

Ms. V. fell to her knees, completely spent. Her virtue was gone. A small hand appeared in her line of sight. She followed the hand up the arm to see the person who was offering her help and frowned. Merissa Dokes? She wasn't supposed to be here. She'd already prayed her through, hadn't she? There was an inner glow that got brighter as Ms. V. watched until she had to cover her eyes.

This time, when she felt the familiar tugging in her center, Ms. V. was ready. She had fought the good fight. She had finished her course and kept the faith. She had brought the last soul home and now she could rest.

Ms. V. turned to see familiar brown eyes also watching her and smiled at Kevin. She felt as if she were on a precipice. She could decide to take Merissa Doke's hand or let the feeling in her center take her. She was so tired, so weary. She needed help, so she reached out and grabbed Merissa's hand.

***

Each day Madison prayed something would be different. Was this that day? The motionlessness of her best friend weighed on her, though she tried hard to carry only upbeat and healing thoughts with her into the room. It had been hard. She missed her friend. She missed the extraordinary woman of God who could quote and apply scripture to any situation.

Madison believed Ms. V. could hear her and those that came to sit and talk to her. She didn't know how. There was no outward sign that Ms. V. was listening, but Madison could feel her friend's awareness.

"Like I said, I might have some good news for you," Dr. Newton said removing his glasses and beginning to wipe them.

"Toward the end of yesterday, your friend's monitor was showing some odd readings. I don't have to tell you how grave things looked after her third week here with very little brain activity. You also know that over the last month the activity has gradually changed for the good until yesterday." He shook his head as if perplexed before continuing. "We aren't really sure how to read the numbers we have been getting on Ms. Vacherchesse's brain activity, but I choose to take it as a positive sign."

Madison's hand came to her chest instinctively, as if the action could keep her heart from beating through her breastbone. What was he saying?

"There is still so much we don't know when it comes to brain injuries, but I always took it as a good sign that Ms. Vacherchesse dreamed."

Madison was startled by his statement. "Dreamed. She dreams?"

"Yes, we started picking up activity, and we noticed that her eyes would move back and forth – a sign of being in a R.E.M. cycle – during the early mornings." His words were matter-of-fact. "Since last evening Ms. Vacha…Vacherchesse.'s vitals have been fluctuating. At first, I was concerned that her body might be giving out. We see that in patients that have been in a coma for an extensive amount of time. Their vitals rise as if the body is giving one last push then everything drops, and the organs fail. As I monitored Ms. Vera...Vacherchesse through the night--"

"Don't hurt yourself," Madison said. "That's why we all call her Ms. V. You have my permission to do the same."

"Well, ah, thank you," he said slowly, having been caught off-guard. Then he continued.

"Ever since she was brought in, I have been communicating and sharing her medical timeline with a number of neurological specialists, and they are almost as baffled as I am. None of them have seen anything to parallel what has been going on with your friend.

"I am telling you this because you are here almost every day, so if you see any obvious changes in her appearance or behavior, I ask that you get a nurse's attention as soon as possible."

Madison started nodding even before he finished his sentence. "Yes, of course."

"Very good." Dr. Newton gestured over to the display. "It's rare for a person who has been in a coma for her length of time to still receive this number of gifts. She must really be loved."

Madison followed his gaze to the table then turned back to him. "Yes. She is very much loved and missed." Madison responded.

"She's a school counselor, right?" Dr. Newton asked as he walked closer to one of the monitors.

"Yes."

"I really liked my counselor as well. He was able to provoke thought with one sentence. It used to get me how he was able to do so much in one thirty-minute session. I think I will always remember him." The doctor gave Ms. V. one more look over then nodded at Madison before leaving the room.

Madison sat with Ms. V. longer than usual. She hoped Ms. V. would show some signs of stirring, but though her eyes moved back and forth as Dr. Newton had described, there was no other movement, and a few minutes before Madison left, even that stopped.

***

Madison was tired and it wasn't surprising. She'd had a long day. She'd had three months of long days. She walked into her apartment and straight to the kitchen where she set the to-go container of egg drop soup down. She had been cold lately, and it wouldn't do to be under the weather. It would keep her from seeing her friend.

She put her purse and bag of student papers on the left side of the kitchen table and sat down on the right. She unfolded the bag, pulling out a spoon wrapped in plastic, a Styrofoam container, and napkins. Since it was just her, she didn't feel the need to put the soup in a bowl. It would be easier to clean up if she just ate it straight out of the container.

She sat there hovering over her soup, thinking how wonderful it would be to see her friend open her eyes, speak a few words, smile at her. Though she now had a daily routine of going to the hospital in the morning and coming to school in time for her five classes instead of spending first period and homeroom grading papers. In a way, it had caused her to be more efficient with her time. Once she got home, she didn't sit and watch television after dinner. She would grade the papers of the day, shower and be in bed by nine-thirty at the latest. She'd wake up at six a.m. and do some stretches as she prayed and meditated on the Lord (if only Ms. V. could see her now). Her friend had been trying to get her to start some type of exercise or stretching regiment for the longest time. Once Madison was done, she would eat a leisurely breakfast and be at the hospital in time for visiting hours to begin.

Some would say she put her life on hold for her friend, but she didn't see it that way. She was there for her friend, and when she woke up, they would resume life together.

Madison finished what she was going to eat of her soup and put the rest in the refrigerator. She went back to her kitchen table, pulled the small stack of papers towards her and began the task of grading.

Two hours later, Madison cut off the light in the kitchen and made her way to the back of her apartment with her phone in hand. She kept it with her always. She never knew when the hospital would call. Since she and Ms. V. had no one else, they had made each other their emergency contacts.

Madison took her shower and was in bed way before nine-thirty. Tonight, the fatigue in her muscles was weighing her down. If she could get eight to nine good hours, she knew she would be able to get through tomorrow.

Chapter 24

For I know the thoughts that I think toward you, saith the LORD, thoughts of peace, and not of evil, to give you an expected end.
1 Corinthians 15:52

"I love you and I am where I belong."

The mist surrounding Madison swirled and her attention was caught by the shapes it made until the sun's rays heated through it. When everything was clear she looked in front of her and caught sight of Beatrice walking toward her. There was a light behind her that made it hard to make out her features, but she knew her friend's walk.

Beatrice moved closer until she was standing right in front of Madison. It had been a long time since she'd seen her friend look so good.

"Hi, my friend."

Madison smiled. It was so good to hear Beatrice's voice.

"Hi, my friend," Madison replied.

Beatrice looked at her for a moment before looking away. "There were a lot of battles fought here. And I'm happy to say most of them were won. God has been both merciful and faithful," Beatrice turned back to Madison.

The look of love on Beatrice's face that reverberated through Madison was almost overpowering, but Madison wouldn't take her eyes off her friend, who began to glow brighter.

"I've fought long and hard for these children, as have you, but my time is up. I've gotten my reward and it is more beautiful than

I ever could have imagined." Beatrice smiled again, and it took Madison's breath away. Her friend's smile felt like peace and joy.

"We won't see each other for a long time, but know this," Beatrice continued. "I love you, and I am where I belong. I am happy, and for now the children are safe, but there will be more. If you're up to it, ask God for the opportunity to fight for them. You won't regret it." Madison more than heard Beatrice's words; she felt them, and understood in an instant what she was being offered. It was a huge responsibility, fighting for children's souls. After all, the battle is not ours, it is the Lord's.

Beatrice didn't turn, but Madison could feel the distance growing between them.

"I love you, Beatrice, and I miss you every day," Madison said, wishing she could do something to keep her friend close for a little longer.

"Yes, I know. But you won't be alone for long. Blessings are upon you." Then the light that suffused Beatrice caused Madison to close her eyes.

When she opened them again, she was in her bedroom, in the dark, with predawn light casting shadows on the ceiling. Madison lay there waiting for her heart rate to return to normal. As she did, a feeling of love passed through her that was so pure it made her shudder and tears formed in her eyes. She couldn't help but smile when Beatrice's scent of lavender and cocoa butter enveloped her, but in the next moment both the feeling and scent were gone, and the room was starker than ever.

Madison jumped out of bed and raced to the bathroom, where she rushed through her morning routine. She dressed in record time, grabbed a banana and an apple and slung her bag of paperwork over her shoulder. She felt an urgency to get to the hospital. She told herself that she had just been dreaming, but she was having a hard time convincing herself.

Madison forced herself to adhere to the speed limit and other rules of the road, but she felt like she was going to miss something if she didn't get to the hospital in the next few minutes.

She had gotten out of her car and was sprinting across the parking lot when her phone began to buzz. She checked it and saw that it was coming from the nurse's station. She answered the call.

"Hello?"

"Hello, is this Madison Marino?" a woman's voice said.

"Yes. I'm walking in right now. I will see you in a moment."

Madison decided to take the stairs because she just couldn't keep still long enough to take the elevator. Her phone reception was poor in the stairwell, so she stopped concentrating on what the woman was saying and raced up the stairs until she reached the third floor.

She walked down the long hall, breathing hard, and made a left as she usually did. She walked to Beatrice's room to find the door open and her bed empty. Hope sparked in her heart. Maybe they had been calling to tell her Beatrice had awakened and were running tests? She left the room, her heart beating almost as fast as it had been when she was running up the stairs. She shook her head to stop the line of thought and went to the nurse's station.

She spoke to the first person that was available. "Hi. I am Beatrice Vacherchese's friend. She's not in her room. I was wondering if maybe she woke up. Her doctor said that she had been exhibiting signs of improvement, and thought she would wake up soon. Are they running tests?"

The nurse held up a hand to stop Madison's barrage of questions.

"Ms. Marino. If you would give me one moment…"

"That's okay, Lucille. I will take it from here." Madison turned around to see Dr. Newton walking up to her. She searched his face, but couldn't find any answers in his expression. She opened her mouth to repeat her questions, but he stopped her.

"Will you come with me?"

Madison followed him down the hall a little ways with trepidation. He opened the door to a small office and gestured for her to sit down. Instead of going round to the other side of the desk in the room he just leaned against it.

"I'm sorry to have to tell you that Ms. Vacherchesse passed away at five forty-six this morning." The words "I'm sorry…" hit Madison like a punch to the gut and destroyed any hope she had left of seeing her friend alive. The roaring in her ears drowned out whatever else Dr. Newton was saying. It didn't really matter in the whole picture, but there was one question that came to her during his explanation for why her best friend was no longer with them. She interrupted him to voice it while she could get words around the growing lump in her throat.

"Did she suffer?"

"I don't believe so. She never woke up from the stroke. But you know the heart attack she suffered afterward made her recovery an even harder feat."

The sob the erupted from Madison startled her, but it didn't stop the next one or the one after that. Inside of seconds she was being racked by uncontrollable sobs. She didn't care that she was getting tears all over her top and pants or that she probably looked a mess. Her friend was gone, and this world was suddenly so much darker.

A few minutes went by before she heard Dr. Newton's voice again. There was a box of tissues placed in her lap, but she didn't use them immediately.

"Is there someone who can come get you?"

"I…I…I…was the someone. I was her someone and she was mine." Madison heard her words and the enormity of them hit her in the chest. Beatrice was alone. She cried for herself and all of the children that wouldn't get to benefit from her wisdom.

"You can't drive. You are too distraught. You said the two of you worked together. Is there someone from the school who could give you a ride home?"

Madison tried to get a handle on her grief, but each of the doctor's questions just reinforced the fact that she was all by herself. There were plenty who had commiserated with her and come to visit Bea at the hospital, but she didn't have anyone's personal number. When she made updates about Bea's progress it was usually through the school office. She preferred to go through her more personal struggles alone, and that was exactly where she found herself now.

"No. No one," she replied before a new wave of tears made her incoherent.

"I'm concerned for you, Ms. Marino. If you're unable to gain some control of yourself I will be forced to admit you." His words shocked her into making more of an effort to master her emotions.

"I'm going to give you a few minutes. If you think you can make your way to the lobby, I will personally call you a cab. You can come back later for your car. I don't need you back here on a gurney. You may also go to the chapel if you'd like. If you think that would help." His tone was firm and demanded attention.

Madison's shoulders shook and the tears continued to flow despite the box of tissues she had made a serious dent in.

He left the room, and Madison sat there feeling dejected. Bea hadn't woken up, he'd said. She'd finished her dreams and transitioned. She tried hard to find some solace in the fact that if anyone went from her bed and walked straight into heaven, Bea had. Her relationship with God was one Madison had found enviable, until Bea told her not to be envious, just make sure her own relationship with God was strong. And though it hadn't happened overnight, Madison was feeling more confident in her relationship with God.

Madison began praying in the midst of her tears. Her silent petitions for comfort grew into quiet pleading for help with the pain in her heart. She burst into sobs again, hugging herself and rocking back and forth until there was a shift in the room, and she thought someone had entered while she was having her mini-breakdown. She worked hard to gain some semblance of control over her emotions. She took Dr. Newton's threat of admittance seriously.

Madison finally looked up through her tears, but no one was in the room to match the presence she felt. The faint scent of lavender and cocoa butter wafted around her, tempting her to fall into another fit of sobs, but the peace that enveloped her stopped the onslaught with a shudder. She straightened in her seat and closed her eyes, trying to absorb the feeling. The feeling of comfort and her friend. It triggered a memory now that her pain wasn't so overwhelming, and she went back to the dream she'd had that morning. Her friend had come to say goodbye. Bea hadn't just left her and transitioned on. She'd said goodbye.

Beatrice's words came over her like a wave. "I love you and I am where I belong." Madison replayed them over and over again in her head and pulled from them the strength she needed to walk out of the room and hold a conversation with enough calmness to convince Dr. Newton that she could drive herself home.

As Madison stood at the nurse's desk, one of the nurses who regularly attended Bea handed her a bag. "These are Ms. V's personal effects. Some of her gifts are also in there, but I threw the flowers away." Madison nodded. She had forgotten about the gifts, and was glad she didn't have to spend what little energy she had left wrapping everything up.

"Thank you," she replied as she took the bag, then turned and made her way from the hospital.

Chapter 25

Blessed be the God and Father of our Lord Jesus Christ, who hath blessed us with all spiritual blessings in heavenly places in Christ: Ephesians 1:3

"Blessings *are* upon you."

Madison had hoped that day would be the worst day of her bereavement for her friend, but it wasn't. There were hard days and less hard days for many months. Beatrice's funeral was a hard day, and so was the beginning of the cleaning out of her home, but Madison had made sure to enlist help from staff and a few former students in that endeavor, and sharing her pain along with good memories started the healing process for her.

Thursday nights were hard, but when the pain became almost unbearable, she would remember her friend's last words, including the recently revived memory of Beatrice's slight change in her favorite saying, "Blessings *are* upon you."

The new school year brought with it some bittersweet memories of walking the halls with her friend. It also brought a new counselor. Mr. Robert Holman came with plenty of degrees, but also a ready smile and curiosity about Ms. V. and how she did things. He thought the best way to serve the students was not to make them fully adapt to him, but for him to adapt to them. Being an expert on all that was Ms. V., Madison spent a lot of time answering questions and asking a few of her own. Mr. Holman was a humble man with a love for God that warmed her heart. She herself could not have picked a better person to step into Ms. V.'s shoes. The fact that Mr. Holman was good-looking was only considered a small benefit in her book.

As the months went by, there was something else she remembered; the field and the children. Once she understood *that* part of the dream and what Beatrice meant as an opportunity to take up the sword, she began to pray to God for clarity and received answers in the way of incidents, situations and small things she would observe about the children in the school. She read books that the Holy Spirit prompted her to read and studied spiritual warfare and demonic forces, making sure to keep in mind that God, Jesus and the Holy Spirit always had the last word and would use her if she made herself available. She saw as she gained insight that friend had been much more than a school counselor. She had been a prayer warrior.

Madison thought over the decision, knowing the responsibility of these children's spiritual lives would weigh heavily on her, but she soon found that she didn't have a choice. Her love for God, love for children, and love for her friend would not let her walk away. So, she took a few days off and sequestered herself in her home, fasting and praying and finally taking on the mantle of prayer warrior. In that moment she could imagine Bea giving her a shoulder bump and a smile and telling her to go for it. Her girl may no longer be with her in the natural, but the work would go on, through her.

***

The sword in her hand felt heavy, but the hilt fit in her hand as if it were made for her. Madison walked onto the mud-covered field and felt the shudder of the ground beneath her. In front of her there was a line of children whose backs were turned to the field.

They were backing up in fright at the demons advancing on them from the sidelines. There was something off about the demons. Every few seconds she could see light shine through them. They were assumptions and fears of what could be. Not of what actually was. She understood. Trepidation and apprehension were weapons used to keep people grounded in situations even when those situations weren't good for them.

Madison called out two of the children she recognized as freshman of the high school class, causing the students to turn around. Hope sparked in their eyes, and that was all she needed.

Madison raised her sword and let out a war cry that drowned out the shrieking coming from the other side. She called for the authority of the Holy Spirit to go in front of her and charged with a smile in her heart. They didn't know whose they were up against, but they would find out soon enough. For she was a fighter in the natural, and God had used her boldness to give her authority where she walked, and the confidence to stand in her rightful place in the army of the Lord.

Epilogue

Well done, thou good and faithful servant: thou hast been faithful over a few things, I will make thee ruler over many things: enter thou into the joy of thy lord.
Matthew 25:21

Well done, thou good and faithful servant:

The feeling that went through her was unlike any pull back to her reality that she'd felt. But the warmth that encompassed her kept her from growing fearful of what was happening to her.

Ms. V. opened her eyes to see herself hovering over the battlefield. There were dark forms lying on the ground in shreds or pieces, and as she rose from the ground she was able to see the entire field. The children that had been rescued began moving away together, holding and hugging one another in a show of solidarity, and she smiled before she was taken higher and higher, and eventually too far up to make out the field.

Ms. V. looked up again at Merissa Dokes but the girl had morphed into a shapeless bright light. It was odd because Ms. V. could still feel her hand wrapped in the girl's hand. She blinked at the light as they continued to ascend, and she felt weightless. Not just in body, but emotionally as well. It was as if many of the pains from her past had melted away in the presence of the intense light. Her failed marriage, all of the things she didn't say to her ex-husband, and the pain from carrying a baby she never got to hold in her arms fell away. She wondered if she would be able to see her child again, and before she finished the thought, she was in a quiet space filled with an overwhelming peace. She sensed, more than saw a being approach her. The closer they came, the more love she felt, until it was all-consuming and all she could feel was the love. Her baby. Her baby had just walked into her arms. She couldn't make out any features, but she recognized their spirit and wept in overwhelming joy. She was home. She was finally home.

Without a reference for time, Ms. V. couldn't say how long it had taken to get from what she took to be a welcoming place to another level of eternity. It couldn't be measured with her eyes, but there was a deep knowing within her that spoke of a closeness that grew with intensity as she moved forward with her daughter, Victoria. Though her daughter never breathed outside of her womb on earth, Ms. V. had known her, loved her, and had given her a name. She had spoken to Victoria for months as she nurtured and sent her all the love she could. She felt that love reflected back at her from Victoria now. It was accompanied by a boundless joy that danced around and through both of them as they continued to move closer to the core of …everything.

Ms. V. moved into the essence of someone familiar and her proverbial heart skipped a beat. Her mom shimmered before her and the happiness threatened to overwhelm every other feeling Ms. V. was experiencing. If she could have cried, the tears would be falling in earnest. *Her mom.* The thought came to her on a sigh and her whole being smiled. She was truly in heaven.

Another light moved from behind the spirit she recognized as her mother. It was bold and comforting in a protective and reliable way. *Dad.* Years of pain from missing her parents slipped away. The memories remained but the loneliness, loss and grieving didn't take her breath away or leave her bereft. It was all a part of her, and welcoming, because she had her parents and child in front of her and surrounding her. What a beautiful reunion. What a ... splendid? Glorious? There were no words to describe the awesomeness of this place and the feelings of wellbeing it brought her.

Ms. V. was now even more grateful for the time she'd spent on Earth getting to know God. Her relationship with Him, His Son, and the Holy Spirit was a mere foretaste of what she was experiencing now, and she understood what Jesus meant when He told those who believed that the Kingdom of God was at hand.

Though time seemed far beyond her reach here, her memories of the love God poured on her during her times of need, praise and worship, as well as when ministering to others, was much clearer now. It was as if someone pulled away the veil that dimmed or turned down the intensity of His love because her body wouldn't have been able to take it. Now that she was in her spiritual form, she felt Him and His love all around her, through her, - and all the sudden immediately in front of her.

The light of Him illuminated the space around her, but He himself was Magnificent. It was as close to a word in English she could find to describe both Him and the feelings He evoked, if she called on what she remembered. If she were to use her heavenly language, she wouldn't use anything less than Hallelujah! God deserved no less when she thought of Him, but so much more as she faced Him. She lowered her head in reverence and praise for being thought worthy enough to be redeemed and admitted into heaven, let alone stand before Him.

Lift up your head and let me look upon you, daughter. She raised her head in obedience and absorbed His warmth. *You have made me proud.* Her whole being smiled at His words.

The brilliance of his light grew until it surrounded her and the others around her.

Thank you for standing in representation and taking care of my children, Dear One. Well done, thou good and faithful servant: thou hast been faithful over a few things, I will make thee ruler over many things: enter thou into the joy of thy Lord.

His light shown even brighter, enveloping her in love, and Ms. V. rejoiced, consumed by Him, elated to be in her Father's arms.

~To Eternity

If you wish to go back and experience Ms. V.'s journey on a more natural path you p may go to page 185

Referenced scriptures from Chapter 18

1. Luke 10:19
2. Romans 8:31a
3. Romans 8:31b
4. 1 John 4:4
5. James 4:7
6. Is. 54:17
7. Matt. 18:18-19
8. Rom. 12:21
9. John 8: 32
10. Deut. 28:7
11. John 16:33
12. John 10:10
13. 2 Thess. 3:3
14. Ps. 91:1-2

Dear Reader

A personal thank you for taking the time out to purchase and read this phenomenal book. I pray you found this book to be a great read for you, as much as it was for me while working on the project. It has been an absolute Holy Ghost filled; God-driven project to work alongside my co-author. I truly believe the Lord united us to tell such a story like this and kept us with one accord during the entire two plus years of collaborating on this dynamic project; always keeping you, the reader's best interest at heart.

My prayer is that you enjoyed reading about the journey of these fascinating characters. After completion of this book, my hope is that it will provoke biblical conversations, and provide spiritual growth.

Prayerfully, you will continue to share this book with others. We greatly appreciate it ;-)

It was such an honor and great experience for me to work on this project in collaboration with co-author Traci. My desire for you, dear reader, is encouragement and inspiration for the coming days, months, and years. I truly believe the best is yet to come.

Sincerely,
D. Tina Batten

Until next time,
Keep reading and expand your dreams,
Traci Wooden-Carlisle

Acknowledgments

From D. Tina Batten

To my hubby, "love you babe." Mom, sister, and children, **you are my heart**. Family and dear friends (too many to name, you know who you are) your undeniable support and encouragement fuel my passion of storytelling. To my pastors and first ladies, past and present, your prayers continue to cover me while in the trenches and valley lows. Please don't stop! I solicit your continued prayers now and for always.

Lastly, to my co-author Traci, we chuckled like children, gave each other virtual high-fives and fist bumps when something great happened. We maintained the task at hand, overcoming sickness, loss of loved ones and keeping the faith during the uncertainties of a worldwide pandemic. Thank you for taking the lead and for seamlessly blending our two voices into one united voice. You were the perfect person to partner on this endeavor. I praise God for you my spiritual sister in Christ. We did it! We completed the assignment together.

From Traci Wooden-Carlisle

To my 'favorite-five', David, Mommy, Daddy, Kerri and Daisia, your support and love is immeasurable. To my mothers and sisters in Christ, there is no way I could have envisioned these places without our talks. Thank you.

Tina, you are my girl! For over two years we've laughed, cried, worshipped God, worked and reworked this storyline and I am proud of what we have accomplished.

To Nicole, Dionne, Neisha, Aziza, BriAnna, Crystal, Joy, Cathy, Holly, Audrey, and Allison, keep dreaming, laughing, praying and walking in the beauty that you are.

About the Authors

D. Tina Batten

D. "Tina" Batten is a loving mother, wife, sister, daughter and Mima to her grandchildren. She is a gifted visual storyteller who is passionate about bringing encouraging messages of inspiration and hope to the world.

Tina Batten, a writer for over eighteen years of various dramatic works of performing art via stage, and film, encompasses unique ways of creating fascinating story concepts that touch the heart of most who view or read her work. She is both honored and thrilled to have teamed up with long-time friend, sister in the gospel and co-author Tracy on this phenomenal collaborative book project. With such a humble heart and desire to bring people together in love and unity, Tina Batten will continue her work as a visual storyteller spreading the good news of Jesus Christ one project after the other.

As Always, D. "Tina" Batten gives God All the Glory!

You can find her at the following social media platforms:

Website: http://www.sisterbatten.com
Facebook Page: https://www.facebook.com/Sister-BattenCom-Sister-Batten-Productions-157650117630075/
FB: Tina Batten
Profile: https://www.facebook.com/tina.batten.18

IG: https://www.instagram.com/sisterbatten/
Twitter: https://twitter.com/sisterbatten
Subscribe to Sister Batten YouTube Channel
shorturl.at/lsxA4
Walking in the Spirit Trailer
https://vimeo.com/ondemand/sisterbattenfilms
If Not For The LORD, Where Would I Be? Delicious Episode
Trailer
https://vimeo.com/ondemand/sisterbattenproductions

Traci Wooden-Carlisle

Traci Wooden-Carlisle began writing to publish in 2011 and enjoys writing stories that provoke thought and evoke emotions. Her desire is to draw readers into the lives of her characters and share messages of God's love, His faithfulness and peace. The messages in her books speak to her way before they speak to her readers.

Traci lives in San Diego with her husband, David. When she isn't writing she does some light traveling or assists people with their physical fitness, creates graphics, designs pretty things for her jewelry business and swag for authors.

You can find her on the following social media platforms.

Website: www.tawcarlisle.com
Newsletter: www.tawcarlisle.com/subscribe
Amazon:http://www.amazon.com/Traci-Wooden
    Carlisle/e/B00OIAS208/
Goodreads:https://www.goodreads.com/Author_TraciWCarlisle
Facebook: www.facebook.com/traciwoodencarlisle
Instagram:_www.instagram.com/tawcarlisle
Bookbub:https://www.bookbub.com/authors/traci-wooden-carlisle
Twitter: www.twitter.com/traciwcarlisle
Pinterest: www.pinterest.com/tawcarlisle

Made in the USA
Las Vegas, NV
15 October 2022

57328669R00144